Looking for JACKIE

Lookin

JA

g for
CKIE

American Fashion Icons
BY KATHLEEN CRAUGHWELL-VARDA

A Fair Street/Welcome Book

Hearst Books

New York

Produced by Fair Street Productions and Welcome Enterprises, Inc.
Susan Wechsler, Alice Wong, *Project Directors*
Deborah Bull, Susan Wechsler, *Project Editors*
David McAninch, *Text Editor*
Gregory Wakabayashi, *Designer*
Robin Raffer/Photosearch, Inc., *Photo Researcher*
Shaie Dively, *Photo Coordinator*

Library of Congress Cataloging-in-Publication Data

Craughwell-Varda, Kathleen.
    Looking for Jackie: American fashion icons / by Kathleen Craughwell-Varda.
        p.   cm.
    ISBN 0-688-16726-8
    1. Clothing and dress.   2. Fashion.   3. Celebrities.   I. Title
TT507.C84   1999
391' .2'0973—dc21   99-29437
                                                                   CIP

Printed in Singapore

First Edition

1 2 3 4 5 6 7 8 9 10

A Fair Street/Welcome Book

www.williammorrow.com

Every attempt has been made to obtain permission to reproduce material protected by copyright. Where omissions may have occurred, the producers will be happy to acknowledge this in future printings.

The producers wish to acknowledge the many individuals and institutions who provided us with illustrations and support:

Front jacket (top left): *Elizabeth Patterson Bonaparte*, Francois J. Kinson, 1817. Maryland Historical Society, Baltimore. Front jacket (middle left): Grace Kelly. The Kobal Collection. Front jacket (bottom left): Bustier for Madonna by Jean Paul Gaultier. Neil Selkirk. Front jacket (right): Jacqueline Kennedy. The Arthur B. Rickerby Photo Collection. Back jacket (background): Design by Adrian for Joan Crawford. Photofest. Back jacket (top right): Katharine Hepburn. Clarence S. Bull/Photofest. Back jacket (middle right): Alice Roosevelt Longworth. Frances Benjamin Johnston/Library of Congress. Back jacket (bottom right): Wallis Warfield Spencer Simpson. Corbis/Bettman-UPI.

Archive Photos: 17 Morgan Collection; 33. Author's Collection: 80; 111. Bibliothèque Nationale de France, Paris: 108; 115 *Elizabeth P. Bonaparte*, Gilbert Stuart. Corbis/APF: 198; 201 (B). Corbis/Bettmann: 89; 120; 123 (L). Corbis/Bettmann-UPI: 8; 16; 27; 28; 31 (B); 34; 99; 117; 118; 126 (T); 137; 138; 139; 141; 180; 200 (B and Behind). Culver Pictures, Inc.: 78; 79; 82 (ML) and (T); 87 (L); 95; 96 (R); 97 (L); 130; 151; 152; 153; 160; 162 (B and Behind); 163; 164; 165 (R); 166; 167; 168 (M); 169; 173; 185; 187; 188 (L); 189; 193. Fair Street Pictures: 91 (TR); 94 (R). Courtesy FIT: 119; 165 (L). Globe Photos: 199 (R) Photograph by Sonia Moskowitz; 199 (L) Photograph by James M. Kelly; 201 (T) Photograph by Lynn McAfee; 203 (L) Photograph by Lisa Rose; 203 (M) Photograph by Richard Chambury; 203 (T) Photograph by Lisa Rose; 204 (R) Photograph by Fitzroy Barrett. Hershenson-Allen Archive: 168 (B); 176 (M); 177; 188 (M); 190 (M). Independence National Historical Park: 42; 43. The James Buchanan Foundation for the Preservation of Wheatland: 66; 71. Courtesy John F. Kennedy Library: 20; 21; 24; 31 (T). The Kobal Collection: 128; 142; 192 (R). Library of Congress: 46 (T); 56; 63; 64; 77; 85; 86 Photograph by Frances Benjamin Johnston; 90; 97 (R). Life Magazine © Time Inc.: 29 (Front Image) Photograph by Yale Joel; 30 (TR) Photograph by Yale Joel; 140 (T) Photograph by Howell Conant. Maryland Historical Society, Baltimore: 46 (B) *Drawing for a Chair for the President's House*, Benjamin Henry Latrobe, 1809; 101 *Elizabeth Patterson Bonaparte*, Francois J. Kinson, 1817; 106 (B) *Jerome Bonaparte*, Isabey, early 19th Century; 106 (T) *Mrs. William Patterson and Daughter, Elizabeth*, Robert Edge Pine, 1785; 112 *Bonaparte, MME. Jerome (Elizabeth Patterson)*, Firmin Massot, 1823; 113; Max Polster Archive: 6; 7; 91 (TL); 98; M-G-M (Courtesy Kobal): 191 (B); 191 (T). Museum of the City of New York: 54 "The Rose of Long Island," *Miss Julia Gardiner and Gentleman in Front of Bogert & McCauley's, No. 86 Ninth Avenue*, Alfred E. Baker, 1840. Gift of Miss Sarah Gardiner. (39.5); 148 *Portrait of Ethel Barrymore in Captain Jinks of the Horse Marines*, Sigismond Daivanowski. Gift of Ethel Barrymore (53.205); 149 Gift of Mr. and Mrs. Spencer Merriam Berger; 150 Gift of Samuel Colt; 154; 155 Photo by Savoy; 156 (T) Gift of Harold Friedlander (68.80.13269); 156 (B) Gift of Mr. and Mrs. Spencer Merriam Berger (50.178.364); 157 *Portrait of Ethel Barrymore*, James Montgomery Flagg, undated. Gift of the artist. Courtesy, Museum of Fine Arts, Boston: 45 *Quaker Meeting*, c. early 19th Century. Bequest of Maxim Karolik; 47 *The Tea Party*, Henry Sargent, c. 1824. Gift of Mrs. Horatio A. Lamb in memory of Mr. and Mrs. Winthrop Sargent. © Collection of the New-York Historical Society: 51 *Dolley Madison*, Bass Otis (attributed to Ezra James) ca. 1817. (accession no. 1867.308); 81 *Poster*: The J.M. Brunswick & Balke Co., shows women playing billiards, from the Bella C. Landauer Collection (neg. no. 34911); 82 (MR) *China Platter with Portrait of Mrs. Grover Cleveland* (neg. 37951). Photofest: 131; 132; 133; 136 (L); 161; 162; 168 (T); 170; 174 (L); 176 (B and Behind); 178; 179 (TL) and (B); 181; 182; 188 (R); 192 (L). Private Collection: 58 (T); 59; 67; 70 (B); 87 (R); 91 (B). Smithsonian Institution: 49; 58 (B); 83. © Vogue/Conde Nast Publications Inc.: 18 Photograph by Richard Rutledge; 116 Photograph by Cecil Beaton; 122 (R) Photograph by Cecil Beaton; 124 (R) Photograph by Cecil Beaton; 125 (R); 127. The White House Collection, copyright The White House Historical Association: 40; 52; 55 *John Tyler*, George P. A. Healy, 1858; 70 (T) *Miss Lane's Reception*, Albert Berghaus, c. 1860.

14 The Arthur B. Rickerby Photo Collection; 26 (R) By permission, Dover Publications, *John F. Kennedy and His Family Paper Dolls* by Tom Tierney; 26 (L) Courtesy of Oleg Cassini Inc.; 29 (Behind) Courtesy The Franklin Mint; 30 (B) Courtesy National Archives; 30 (TL) From the collection of Harvey Goldberg; 44 *Le Cafe Frascati*, Philibert Louis Debucourt, 1807. Musee dela Ville de Paris, Musee Carnavalet, Paris, France. Giraudon/Art Resource, NY; 50 *Dolley Payne (Madison)*, Anonymous. Collections of The Virginia State Historical Society, Richmond, VA; 60 *Howe's Complete Ball-Room Handbook*. From the Collections of Henry Ford Museum & Greenfield Village; 68 *The Grand Staircase at Buckingham Palace, July 1848*, Eugene Lami. The Royal Collection ©1999 Her Majesty Queen Elizabeth II; 73 *Portrait of Harriet Lane Johnston*, John Henry Brown, 1878. National Museum of American Art, Washington DC/Art Resource, NY; 74 Buffalo & Erie County Historical Society; 82 (B) General Research Division, The New York Public Library, Astor, Lenox, Tilden Foundations; 93 *Reception at the White House (Detail)*, William Baxter Clossen, 1908. Courtesy Sagamore Hill National Historic Site, NPS; 94 (L) *The Black Hat*, Frank W. Benson, 1904. Museum of Art, Rhode Island School of Design; Gift of Walter Callender, Henry D. Sharpe, Howard L. Clark, William Gammell and Isaac C. Bates. Photography by Cathy Carver; 96 (L) Theodore Roosevelt Collection, Harvard College Library; 107 *Elizabeth P. Bonaparte's Wedding Dress*. The Metropolitan Museum of Art, Purchase, Gifts in memory of Elizabeth N. Lawrence, 1983. (1983.6.1) Photograph by Sheldon Collins. Photograph ©1986 The Metropolitan Museum of Art; 109 *Portrait of Madame Recamier*, Francois Gerard (1770-1837). Musee de la Ville de Paris, Musee Carnavalet, Paris/Giraudon/Art Resource, NY; 121 Cecil Beaton/Camera Press Express; 124 (L) Illustration from the archives of Wade Laboissonniere. Reprinted with the permission of The McCall Pattern Company; 125 (L) Courtesy Private Collection; 126 (B) Courtesy Wade Laboissonniere; 134 Courtesy Simplicity Pattern Co. Inc.; 135 Paramount (Courtesy Kobal); 136 (R) Illustration from the archives of Wade Laboissonniere. Reprinted with the permission of The McCall Pattern Company; 140 B *Wedding in Louisville, KY*, Lin Caufield, 1956. University of Louisville Photographic Archives; 158 Photo by Nikolas Muray, courtesy Nikolas Muray Photo Archives. National Portrait Gallery, Smithsonian Institution/Art Resource, N.Y.; 174 (R) Missouri Historical Society; 179 (TR) Catalog page 33 is from the Spring 1933 Sears general catalog. This page is reprinted by arrangement with Sears, Roebuck, and Co. and is protected under copyright. No duplication is permitted; 184 The Ben Carbonetto Collection/Time Inc.; 190 (Behind) RKO (Courtesy Kobal); 190 (B) Columbia (Courtesy Kobal); 196 Neil Selkirk; 201 (M) Sherry Zuckerman; 202 Patrick Demarchelier, Courtesy Harper's Bazaar; 204 (L) Miramax (Courtesy Kobal); 205 Corbis/Pacha.

Foreword

Most of the fascinating and influential American women profiled in this insightful book—from Dolley Madison to Jackie Onassis—came to know fashion through first-hand encounters with Paris, the center of European haute couture. In a centuries-old tradition that began with the patronage of the French court, dressmakers of Paris would, each season, create amazing confections of ornamental detail that brought new variations to the fashionable silhouette. In turn, their illustrious clients, usually eager for novelty, needed little persuasion to adopt the newest fashion. Thus, from the royal halls and later from the salons and exhibitions of European couture houses, new styles would make their way, often in the form of sketches, to the pages of ladies'

magazines. From there, the newest designs, usually in a somewhat less opulent form, would eventually be disseminated throughout the fashionable centers of Europe and America among women of less grand circumstances. Many of these women, when confronted with a dramatically new fashion, would look to a fashion arbiter—perhaps the editor of a favorite fashion magazine, perhaps the local dressmaker with the most cachet, perhaps a prominent public figure—who could offer assurance that adopting a new style would be the correct and proper thing to do. Thus, fashion prior to the 1970s was a discipline, a dictum from above that wafted down through the strata of society, leaving its impression on whomever it touched.

For Americans, the great fashion editors of the nineteenth and twentieth centuries provided the most guidance, even rules. Beginning in the 1830s with Sarah Josepha Hale of *Godey's Lady's Book*, through Carmel Snow of *Harper's Bazaar* and Diana Vreeland's legendary reign at *Vogue*, fashion publishing has never lacked a strong point of view. And by offering rules to follow, fashion doyennes made the average woman feel more comfortable evaluating and adopting the latest trends. As advertising blossomed through the nineteenth century, celebrity endorsements of products—as well as fashions—helped spread fads and fancies. By the late nineteenth century, many famous actresses were posing in the newest styles—the photographs artfully altered at the bosom, waist, or hip to achieve an ideal silhouette. And in a time-honored tradition, the great couture houses of Paris lent additional confidence to those fortunate enough to be their clients. American women shopping at Worth in the nineteenth century or Dior in the mid-twentieth could relax, knowing that each detail was perfectly adjusted to their needs and measurements. As the fashion periodicals grew to rely more and more on haute couture for images of style, the influence of designers such as Chanel, Patou, Vionnet, and Schiaparelli became ever more widely felt.

Yet even a brief look at the storied evolution of American fashion shows that it took more than a successful chemistry between couture and the media to change the course of fashion history. These watershed moments required catalysts, larger-than-life figures who could transcend the rigid fashion hierarchy to give average women the confidence to embrace a new style. It is at this juncture that *Looking for Jackie* astutely and colorfully identifies some of the American women who were looked up to by their more anonymous countrywomen as fashion icons—women whose lives and clothes stood as models of style for the average woman. Serving to emphasize just how ephemeral a fashion moment can be is the fact that several of these very influential ladies are far from household names today. Yet each of them contributed to the onward thrust of fashion in America. Each, in her turn, has staying power—their stories remain as indelible records of the development of what we now call "personal style."

Jean L. Druesedow, Director, Kent State University Museum

Introduction

Two fashion icons of the twentieth century greet each other as Jackie Kennedy welcomes Her Serene Highness, Princess Grace of Monaco, to the White House.

In recent years, the term "icon" has enjoyed such renewed popularity that it verges on overuse. It seems today that virtually any celebrity lucky enough to draw crowds at a movie premiere or to appear on the pages of *People* magazine is instantly dubbed an "icon for her generation." It was thus with a fairly rigid definition in mind that I set out to select a handful of fashionable American women who could bear the full weight of the term—who were, in the truest sense, emblems of their era and objects of public adulation.

I ended up with a relatively small group of women who spanned almost every era of American history. Some are well known, others have been forgotten. All of them, however, share a few notable traits. Each of these women developed a personal style, a look, that was at once inimitable and widely copied, and that in some way permanently altered the American cultural landscape; each of them enjoyed overwhelming acceptance by middle-class women. These figures, in turn, often transcended the world of fashion, capturing our collective imagination and becoming in the process the reigning symbol of a national feminine ideal. Most important, perhaps, is the fact that these women—icons or not—retained a deeply human character. Their lives may have been real-life fairy tales, but their joys, triumphs, and heartbreaks were universal.

Many books have examined the doyennes of fashion and style; most of them, however, have confined their scope to the circumscribed world of haute couture and to that elite group of women who orbited the great fashion houses of Europe. The purpose of this book is to focus attention on a handful of remarkable American women who, intentionally or not, reached out to their respective generations—who were able both to embrace couture and to break through the barriers of class that otherwise would have separated them from average women. What emerges from such an endeavor is not only a set of fascinating biographies, but also a rich visual history of the changing currents of American style.

I first began to explore this topic while studying at the Costume Institute at the Metropolitan Museum of Art in New York. As I began casually to examine the role celebrated women have played in inspiring American fashion trends, I was not surprised to learn how many fashions in the twentieth century were influenced by one woman: Jacqueline Kennedy Onassis. The abundance of critical and popular thought devoted to Jackie's momentous impact on American fashion led me to ponder whether this amazing woman was a cultural anomaly. Or was she only the most visible member of a larger group of women whose mode of dress influenced legions of admirers?

Jackie, I discovered, could serve as a touchstone for a much broader examination of a whole range of American women whose lives and clothes reshaped Americans' approach to fashion. As I assembled my list, adding a name here and eliminating another there, a pattern emerged: the women I selected could be characterized as falling into several broad categories of public life. Some, like Jackie, were women who resided in the White House, serving as First Ladies and official hostesses for the nation's highest office.

Others were what I came to call "women of rank and privilege": American women who, by design or twist of fate, married into the royal families of Europe. And a number of the women, not surprisingly, were stars of the American stage and screen.

Of these three groups, the women who have resided in the White House, in particular the First Ladies, have traditionally inherited the most difficult public role; they were forced to define themselves and their personal style within the strict confines of political acceptability. From the moment a very private Martha Washington reluctantly entered the public arena in 1789, each mistress of the executive mansion has had to cope with an ever-increasing barrage of public attention. As the national press has grown bolder and its power more far-reaching, First Ladies have lost more and more of their privacy.

The select group of women who entered the world of European nobility endured a somewhat different burden. Republican ideals aside, Americans have always had a deep fascination with monarchy—and with all the wealth, pomp, and ceremony that royalty entails. The notion of an American woman winning the affections of a prince or king is nothing short of transfixing, and those few women who have managed to do it have had to live up to all our fairy-tale expectations. Anyone who contends that this collective obsession with royalty has faded in recent years must somehow explain the idolatry that has attended both the life and death of Diana, Princess of Wales.

Virtually no title or public office, however, can claim to have produced more dazzling—and ephemeral—icons than has Hollywood. Beginning with the early stars of the American stage and the heroines of silent film, the entertainment industry has fostered a cult of star worship that now enjoys a virtual monopoly on the American popular consciousness. What these women of the stage and screen may have lacked in personal fashion sense (although this was not easy to judge, because they were so often bedecked in studio-mandated garb) they made up for in sheer physical radiance, which illuminated their faces, clothes, and jewels.

The women featured in this book are as remarkable for their differences as they are for what they have in common. Many were born into privileged families, but others grew up staunchly middle class or even in poverty. Included are social conformists and iconoclasts, traditionalists and feminists, those who avidly sought fame and those who attempted to elude its oppressiveness. Personality aside, each of these women came to embody a sort of feminine ideal—a prototype that somehow contained, even defined, some essential ingredient of womanhood. In this respect, details were less important than the appeal of the whole, and the public was often content to overlook the less irreproachable aspects of these women's lives. Many may have frowned on the Kennedy widow's marriage to a Greek shipping tycoon, but as long as appearances were kept up—as long as she looked fabulous—people continued to adore her. A century and a half earlier, Dolley Madison's wildly devoted admirers seemed equally unperturbed by the middle-aged First Lady's plunging necklines.

It is this organic connection with the public that separates a merely stylish figure from a true fashion icon. The connection may in some cases be built entirely on appearances, but the fact is that these women, intentionally or not, prompted ordinary people to want to take part in their joys and sorrows. By the same token, the styles these women embraced have taken on immense cultural importance. Their clothes are no longer mere exemplars of a prevailing style; they represent a moment in history. Jackie Kennedy's pink Chanel-style suit has become an emblem for her husband's assassination, just as Joan Crawford's padded shoulders and cinched waist are synonymous with late 1930s and early 1940s Hollywood glamour.

From the beginning, the driving force behind this unusual confluence of style, personality, and history has been the media, and it is impossible to understand the lives of these women without a consideration of the role of the press in helping to shape them. Before television, glossy photo spreads, or even newsreels were invented, illustrated newspapers devoted countless pages to the social agendas, wedding trousseaux, and shopping sprees of America's most fashionable women. For instance, in Frances Cleveland's day—the turn of the last century—young women kept scrapbooks containing newspaper clippings of the captivating young First Lady. With the advent of the moving picture, color photography, and television, the elements of style rapidly became part of the national vocabulary, and fashion itself underwent an evolution—from artisanal craft into industry, and from there into a way of life.

This book is by no means a definitive history of the leading figures in American fashion. Rather, it is a colorful account of the way in which fashion has fused with personality in America over the last two centuries— a fusion embodied by Jacqueline Kennedy Onassis and boldly forged by the fashion icons who came before her.

A Wom
Di

an of stinction

4

Jacqueline Kennedy Onassis

The buzz of anticipation was palpable when Jacqueline Onassis entered the Metropolitan Museum of Art for the opening of its costume exhibition *The Age of Napoleon* in 1989. As she walked into the gallery—already filled with celebrities, business moguls, and art patrons—all eyes were on her, the most famous American woman of the last half of the twentieth century. According to an eyewitness, as she moved through the room, the crowd parted as if in the presence of royalty.

Indeed, by that time, Jacqueline Onassis had in many respects become an American monarch—as adored and revered as a princess or queen. At a state dinner, a European nightclub, or a charity event, the reaction was the same: Jackie mesmerized. She possessed a rare patrician beauty that contrasted with the postwar American ideal. She had glamour, in the purest sense of the word. Her impact on popular culture when she arrived on the public scene in 1960 was instantaneous: the dual American ideals of the sultry blonde and the prim, starched girl next door were immediately replaced by that of the cool, sophisticated brunette.

Jacqueline Kennedy Onassis had a sense of fashion that revolutionized the way women looked at clothes. Her confident style encouraged women to embrace the joy of wearing fine clothes and creating an elegant, aristocratic appearance. The formula was simple: tailored clothes with an air of simplicity, fabrics in flattering shades and patterns, accessories used to complement a look, and eye-catching details. Only Jackie's star quality could take such a simple formula and invest it with the power to alter permanently the direction of women's fashion.

Internationally celebrated for her sense of style, Jackie held the world's attention—whether touring the capitals of Europe or visiting India, as shown in the photograph at left.

Jacqueline Lee Bouvier was born into wealth and privilege. Her parents, John Vernou "Black Jack" Bouvier and Janet Lee, were opposites. Known for his swarthy good looks, Black Jack was a womanizer and a spendthrift, while Janet was conservative; having come from modest means, she craved the life of the proper upper-class lady. During the summer of 1929, the Bouviers had left the heat of their New York apartment to spend the weekend at their home in Southampton, Long Island—the summer playground of New York's social elite. There, Jacqueline was born on July 28. Her upbringing followed a course typical of the American upper class: nannies, private schools, dance classes, and riding lessons. And while her childhood had all the outward trappings of happiness, it was scarred by the deterioration of her parents' marriage, which ended in divorce in 1940. Two years later, her mother remarried, and Jackie began to split her time between her parents.

After graduating in 1947 from Miss Porter's, a finishing school in Farmington, Connecticut, Jackie made her official society debut at Hammersmith Farm, her stepfather's home in Newport, Rhode Island. Her traditional white silk gown, with its fitted bodice, small puffed sleeves, and tulle skirt, had been purchased for fifty-nine dollars at a New York department store. At age eighteen, Jackie exuded grace and charm beyond her years. It was this blend of sophistication and glamour that inspired society columnist Cholly Knickerbocker to name her Debutante of the Year. "She has poise, is soft-spoken and intelligent, everything the leading debutante should be," declared Knickerbocker.

Seen here with her parents (below)—a stylish equestrienne even at age five—Jackie's passion for horseback riding would, in her White House years, spark a trend in English riding apparel. At age seven (right), she posed with her Great Dane, King Phar.

That fall, Jackie entered Vassar College in Poughkeepsie, New York, where she majored in literature. After spending two years in rural upstate New York, Jackie escaped to Paris to spend her junior year at the Sorbonne. Having been raised with a passion for books and fine art, Jackie fell in love with France, and in particular with its history and culture. She mastered the language, eventually becoming proficient in Spanish and Italian as well. With much regret, she returned to the States to finish

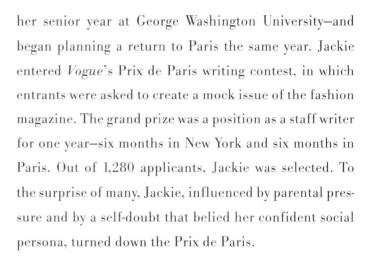

her senior year at George Washington University—and began planning a return to Paris the same year. Jackie entered *Vogue*'s Prix de Paris writing contest, in which entrants were asked to create a mock issue of the fashion magazine. The grand prize was a position as a staff writer for one year—six months in New York and six months in Paris. Out of 1,280 applicants, Jackie was selected. To the surprise of many, Jackie, influenced by parental pressure and by a self-doubt that belied her confident social persona, turned down the Prix de Paris.

With this opportunity behind her, another one soon opened before her. Jacqueline Bouvier was still living at home with her mother and stepfather when she met Congressman John Fitzgerald Kennedy at a dinner party in Georgetown in May of 1951. Even though guests thought they detected a mutual attraction between the two, nothing came of this initial meeting. Then, in 1952, they met again. This time, romance blossomed between Jackie and the recently elected U.S. senator, and they were married on September 12, 1953, in Newport, Rhode Island. Although the bride and her family wanted a small affair, the groom's father, Joseph Kennedy, intervened. More than three thousand spectators watched as the 750 guests filed into the church for the nuptial mass. Afterward, 1,300 guests returned to Hammersmith Farm for an outdoor reception.

The Newport wedding would catapult the former Debutante of the Year from the society page to the front page around the world. For this momentous occasion, Jackie wanted to wear a sleek, modern gown, in keeping with the pared-down style she preferred for both day and evening, but Jack persuaded her to select something more traditional and old-fashioned.

The bride's mother hired Ann Lowe, an African-American dressmaker who catered to society women, to make her gown. An ivory silk taffeta was chosen to

Wearing the clothes that would come to characterize her style, Jackie was twenty-two when she posed for this photo in 1951— the year she won the Vogue Prix de Paris writing contest.

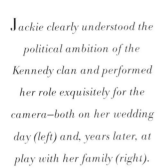

Jackie clearly understood the political ambition of the Kennedy clan and performed her role exquisitely for the camera—both on her wedding day (left) and, years later, at play with her family (right).

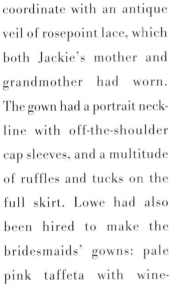

coordinate with an antique veil of rosepoint lace, which both Jackie's mother and grandmother had worn. The gown had a portrait neckline with off-the-shoulder cap sleeves, and a multitude of ruffles and tucks on the full skirt. Lowe had also been hired to make the bridesmaids' gowns: pale pink taffeta with wine-colored satin sashes. A few days before the wedding, a flood in the dressmaker's workrooms, on Lexington Avenue in New York City, destroyed ten of the fifteen gowns, including the wedding gown. Without alerting the bride's family, Lowe and her staff remade the entire order just in time for the wedding. The wedding gown, which had originally taken two months to complete, was recreated in five days.

Jacqueline Bouvier Kennedy married into one of America's wealthiest families, and she began to buy the clothes she had always longed to wear but had been unable to afford. With society friends reporting back to her on the latest styles in New York, Paris, and Rome, Jackie was soon spending as much as twenty thousand dollars a year on clothes. These exorbitant bills drove Jack to distraction, but her response was simple and seductively pragmatic: "I have to dress well, Jack, so I won't embarrass you. As a public figure, you'd be humiliated if I was photographed in some saggy old housedress. Everyone would say your wife is a slob and refuse to vote for you." Indeed, Jackie's investment would soon yield a dividend that few—not even the shrewd Mrs. Kennedy herself—could clearly foresee. With Jack on his way to the nation's highest office, and with Jackie by his side, the tone was set: it would soon become de rigueur for the wives of public figures to pay meticulous attention to their attire and public image.

As the presidential election of 1960 drew near, John F. Kennedy's political advisers were wary of the effect his glamorous wife would have on voters. Jackie was not the average

American homemaker, and many feared that her expensive clothes and aristocratic lifestyle would alienate America's burgeoning middle class. The opposite proved to be true. Jackie was young, fresh, and new—a welcome change from the typical politician's wife. After years of traditional hausfraus such as Bess Truman and Mamie Eisenhower, the public was ready for an exciting presence in the White House: crowd size doubled at campaign stops when Jackie was present. "It turned out that the voters loved her," noted campaign organizer Charles Peters. "She was perceived as the princess, and they basked in her glamour rather than being offended by it." Joseph Cerrell, who later became the executive director of the Democratic Party in California, recalled, "I remember her causing a considerable stir because it was the first time Californians had seen anybody sporting a hemline above the knee. Her glamour and her unconventional beauty attracted attention and enticed the news media, for whom the couple had become a symbol of youth and vitality—a new symbol of a New Age."

During the presidential campaign, Republicans turned Jackie's French couture clothes, and their price tags, into a campaign issue. Pat Nixon's "good Republican cloth coat" was held up as a mark of solidarity with the average American housewife. The attack backfired. Asked by reporters about her spending on clothes, Jackie responded, "That's dreadfully unfair. They're beginning to snipe at me about as often as they attack Jack on Catholicism. I'm sure I spend less than Mrs. Nixon on clothes. She gets hers at Elizabeth Arden, and nothing there costs less than two hundred or three hundred dollars." Apparently, Jackie's famous red cloth campaign coat was merely a copy of a Givenchy original and had been purchased at Ohrbach's department store. Despite Jackie's attempts to downplay her wardrobe, however, the following update appeared in *Women's Wear Daily* in September of 1960, just two months before the election: "Now it can be told—Mrs. John F. Kennedy, wife of the Democratic presidential candidate, has been diplomatically told that for political expediency—'no more Paris clothes, only American fashion.'"

In spite of the public hand-wringing over Jackie's cosmopolitan wardrobe, the Kennedy campaign was receiving strong support from clothing manufacturers and retailers across the country who anticipated the impact her clothes would have on the nation's consumers. *Women's Wear Daily* predicted that Jacqueline Kennedy would be "the most photogenic, fashion-conscious and chic occupant of the White House since Dolley Madison." Setting fears of a middle-class backlash aside, America's fashion industry was ready to gamble that Jackie's wardrobe would become a bellwether for the tastes of thousands of potential consumers.

Shortly after her husband's victory, Jackie gave birth to her son, John. During her recuperation she began to plan her White House wardrobe. Only thirty-one years old, Jacqueline Kennedy was the third-youngest First Lady in American history. As a President's wife and mother of two young children—three-year-old Caroline and newborn John—the pressures and responsibilities were enormous. Her first priority was maintaining a degree of normalcy in her family routine. She recognized the need for appropriate clothes and the importance her mode of dress would play in her husband's presidency. The elegant grandeur that would characterize the Kennedy administration was in fact carefully crafted. The Kennedys set out to represent the perfect American family, and photographers were hired to take meticulously arranged photographs of the first family at "informal" moments. While Jackie protested this invasion of their privacy, the technique succeeded in establishing an unprecedented intimacy between the American public and the office of the President.

In what would become one of many relationships with leading figures of the fashion world, Jackie consulted with Diana Vreeland, then editor of *Harper's Bazaar* (and a formidable doyenne of style in her own right), on her White House wardrobe. As First Lady of the United States, Jackie knew that the politically expedient strategy would be to wear only American-manufactured clothing. As a disciple of French couture, she would of course have to redirect her fashion selections. In turning her focus to her own backyard, however, Jackie unwittingly brought attention to all that was beautiful and stylish in America, reinvigorating a nation's pride in its own rich tradition in the decorative arts. This attentiveness extended famously beyond the world of fashion and design to include the bohemian domain of the cultural elite: artists, writers, and dancers were invited into this new White House, the redecoration of which Jackie had carefully researched and overseen.

Designers from around the country sent letters and sketches, offering their services. Oleg Cassini, a descendant of Russian aristocracy who had designed clothes for many Hollywood celebrities, had been creating and selling his own line of fashions since the 1950s. Cassini was a friend of Jack Kennedy and his father, Joseph, and he sent a note to Jackie asking to be considered for selection as her personal designer. Cassini was allowed to meet with Jackie while she was still recuperating in the hospital after John's birth, and he brought with him several new designs created exclusively for her, including one for a gown for the inaugural ball. "I want you to be the most elegant woman in the world," Cassini told her. "I think that you should start from scratch with a look—a look that will set trends and not follow them."

Cassini's sales pitch worked (thanks in part to Joe Kennedy's offer to pay for all his daughter-in-law's clothes if she chose Cassini). The look the designer proposed was unlike his typical work and borrowed heavily from Givenchy. Together, Cassini and Jackie discussed the impact they wanted her clothes to have. Beneath that famous whispery voice was a woman with an iron will: Jackie knew exactly how she wanted to appear. Working closely with Cassini, she helped craft her image as the best-dressed woman in the world. No detail was too small to escape discussion, and together they scrutinized everything from color and cut to accessories. The style was to be simple, youthful, and elegant, the lines clean and uncluttered, setting off the First Lady's lithe figure. The look they created was the first purely American style to meet with enthusiastic acceptance on the international fashion scene, and it singlehandedly boosted the U.S. fashion industry's worldwide stature.

Soon after she appointed Cassini as her personal designer, Jackie sent him a letter outlining the wardrobe she would require:

What I need are dresses and coats for daytime, dresses suitable to wear to lunch. I don't know if you design coats, but I now see that will be one of my biggest problems, as every time one goes out of the house, one is photographed in the same coat.

Then for afternoon, cocktail dresses suitable for afternoon receptions and receiving lines— in other words, fairly covered up. Also, one or two silk coats to wear over them when I go out in the late afternoon. Any suggestions for accessories you have to wear would also be appreciated.

Then some pretty, long evening dresses suitable for big official dinners. You know the kind I like: a covered-up look. Even though these clothes are for official life, please don't make them dressy as I'm sure I can continue to dress the way I like—simple and young clothes, as long as they are covered up for the occasion.

A fashion purist, Jackie insisted that all her dresses be originals and that any designs intended to be shown as part of Cassini's collection be altered from those of her exclusive commissions. She particularly wanted to avoid seeing "fat little women hopping around in [my] gown[s]."

A problem arose shortly after Cassini was hired. For the inaugural ball, Jackie had already ordered a gown of her own design from Ethel Frankau, the head designer of the fashion salon at Bergdorf Goodman. But Jackie adored the white satin gown Cassini had proposed when they first met. Jackie's solution was to wear Cassini's creation to the inauguration eve gala that was being orchestrated by Frank Sinatra, reserving the Bergdorf's gown for the balls on the night of the inauguration itself.

Jackie, who was only thirty-one years old when John F. Kennedy took office, was much younger and far more stylish than the wives of most Washington politicians (overleaf). An increasingly fashion-conscious public embraced her sleek, modern look and the self-confidence it projected.

*D*esigner Oleg Cassini persuaded Jackie to use him as
her primary designer during the White House years,
and created the famously popular fawn-colored wool
inauguration coat—seen above in Cassini's own
sketch—that defined the Jackie look.

I n the end, the outfit that truly announced the definitive "Jackie look" to the world was the Cassini dress and coat she wore to the inauguration ceremony on the Capitol steps. The ensemble was deliberately understated to highlight Jackie's youth and natural beauty. Cassini designed a fawn-colored wool coat with a sable collar and matching dress. Since every politician's wife would be huddled in furs, Jackie's outfit would create the perfect contrast. Diana Vreeland suggested that Jackie carry a matching sable muff. The now-legendary pillbox hat she wore that day was created by Halston, who was then the custom-design milliner at Bergdorf Goodman's renowned hat department (Jackie had been wearing Halston hats for years). The hat was inspired by a pillbox created by the Hollywood designer Adrian for Greta Garbo in the 1932 film *As You Desire Me*. Halston's version was purposely oversized to accommodate Jackie's bouffant hairstyle, which measured twenty-four inches in diameter when fully coiffed.

The hat was an immediate success. When asked later about its impact, Halston recalled that the day of the inauguration was cold and windy. Met with a gust of wind as she stepped from the limousine, Jackie grabbed her hat, putting a small dent in the crown. News photos picked up this image, and women and milliners began to put dents in their pillbox hats in imitation of the First Lady. Within a few weeks, the pillbox hat was the most popular style in the country. As an Ohrbach's buyer noted in April of 1961, "It's amazing how many women ask for the Kennedy hat. Even older women. They put the hat on the back of their heads, look in the mirror, and you can just see what's going through their minds. They're having the time of their lives seeing themselves as Jackie Kennedy. Naturally, we don't do anything to break the spell."

*T*he vitality of the young Kennedys was captured on a
blustery, cold inauguration day in January of 1961
(right). No one could have gauged the longevity of
Jackie's fashion impact: almost forty years later, her
White House wardrobe would appear in a popular book
of stylish paper dolls (this page).

Although eight months pregnant and in delicate health, the First Lady joined her husband in New York for a round of campaign stops, including a ticker-tape parade through the financial district. The overwhelming enthusiasm of the crowds, which both delighted and frightened her, would continue even after the election.

As First Lady, Jacqueline Kennedy's initial impact on American culture was unequivocally in the realm of fashion. Women were immediately drawn to her chic, elegant appearance and began to emulate her. Clothing manufacturers responded to the demand by having copies of Jackie's clothes in stores within six weeks of their debut. She did not always originate fashions as First Lady, but she had the uncanny ability to detect a stylish trend just as it was emerging and put her stamp on it. Her less-is-more approach to dressing was a refreshing change from the typical fashions of the day. The "Jackie look" derived much of its popularity from its remarkable simplicity, and its components can be easily broken down:

The Shift Dress—Ranging from simple, sleeveless, knee-length linen frocks to more luxurious silk versions, usually with matching, unstructured jackets, the shift dress was a comfortable yet flattering garment that accentuated Jackie's regal posture and narrow hips. She favored boat necklines with bows or buttons as accents.

The Plain Cloth Coat—Sometimes fitted, sometimes cut to the fashionable A-line, Jackie's coats had youthful flair and interesting collars that drew attention to her face. Cassini's designs were made in solid colors, and were often unadorned except for oversized buttons and tassels in the same fabric.

The Pillbox Hat—This hat became a Jackie trademark and was reinterpreted by Marita O'Connor of Bergdorf Goodman's custom hat department in a variety of materials, including wool, silk, fur, and straw. Ironically, neither Jack nor Jackie was fond of hats, although most men and women in the 1950s and 1960s wore them in public. But the presidential couple realized that going hatless would have a negative impact on the millinery industry, and the pillbox and the other millinery creations that Jackie sported were worn to encourage the hat trade. While Jackie chose several flattering styles to wear in her official capacity, Jack elected to carry a hat rather than wear one. "Oh dear it was so pleasant when I didn't have to wear hats," Jackie once wrote to O'Connor. "They will pauperize me and I still feel absurd in them!"

The Bouffant Hairdo—The style that came to define the 1960s was created by Jackie's New York hairdresser, Kenneth Battelle, who soon became the most popular hair stylist in the country. He was flown down to the White House for special occasions. The rest of the time, maintaining Jackie's hairdo was left to her Washington hairdresser, whom she saw four times a week.

In addition to these basic signature components, Jackie also influenced the popularity of low-heeled pumps, one-shoulder evening gowns, tapered, slim-fitting pants, and English riding clothes. (Her sunglasses didn't appear until after her marriage to Aristotle Onassis in 1968, when she increasingly sought shelter from staring eyes.)

Jackie Kennedy's overall impact on the American popular imagination was enormous. A 1960 article in *Life* magazine said, "Fashion ads twinkle more mischievously with Jackie's unmistakable wide eyes. Her bouffant hairdo is becoming a by-word in beauty salons. All in all, the shy, beautiful First Lady's fashion followers are building up quite a bandwagon . . .

A group of Jackie look-alikes sporting the popular pillbox hat. Jackie's famous pearls appear in the background around the photo.

Manufacturers and advertisers all over the country took note of the first family's popular appeal. Commercial exploitation came in a variety of shapes and sizes, from mannequins to bottle stoppers. In the photo below, adoring fans greet the President and First Lady as they leave a Washington theater.

Despite herself, she is becoming the nation's #1 fashion influence." Her image was commercially exploited, too. A Danish firm introduced Jackie mannequins. There were Jackie dolls and cutouts, and her face appeared on a host of kitschy items, including hot plates and planters. A Jackie look-alike opened *The Jack Benny Program* in 1962; the character Jackie Kennelrock soon appeared on *The Flintstones*; and in 1961, Miss America expressed a desire to "be more like Jackie." During her first year in the White House, Jackie received between six thousand and nine thousand fan letters a week, many from young girls.

Jackie's worldwide appeal became further apparent when the Kennedys went to Canada for their first official state visit in May of 1961. Jack Kennedy saw his wife in a

This vivid blue strapless gown (right) was one of Jackie's
favorites. She wore it to the ball at the Breakers in
Newport, Rhode Island, celebrating the 1962 America's
Cup race. In the photo below, Jackie arrives at a state
dinner in France wearing a Cassini-designed floor-length
pink-and-white straw lace gown.

new light as he witnessed her tremendous diplomatic skills and the easy manner with which she charmed foreign dignitaries and the public at large. The trip gave Jackie a needed boost of self-confidence, and it became increasingly obvious that she was a political asset to her husband and his administration on both the domestic and international scenes.

By the time the Kennedys made their state visit to France in 1961, Jackie was already hailed as an international sensation, but the ovation she received upon landing outstripped all expectations. More than a million Parisians lined the parade route, chanting, "Jacqui! Jacqui!" as the Kennedys entered Paris. "From the moment of her smiling arrival at Orly Airport," *Time* magazine reported, "the radiant young First Lady was the Kennedy who really mattered."

The wardrobe Cassini created for the trip to France was designed with two objectives—to make Jackie look like a queen, and to prove that American fashion was the equal of French couture. It worked liked a charm. The normally taciturn Charles de Gaulle was completely enchanted with the First Lady, and the two spent a great deal of time discussing, in French, his country's history. As a courtesy to

the French couture industry, Jackie wore a gown designed for her by Hubert de Givenchy to the state dinner given at Versailles in honor of the President and the First Lady.

Jackie's trip to Europe galvanized her international reputation as one of the world's best-dressed women. She regularly appeared on the covers of international magazines, including many published behind the Iron Curtain. Her projects to promote the arts and her spectacular restoration of the White House prompted Robert Frost to muse, "There have been some great wives in the White House—like Abigail Adams and Dolley Madison—so great you can't think of their husbands, Presidents, without thinking of them. It looks like we're having another one now."

The Kennedys were already making plans for their next four years in the White House when it all came to an abrupt end in Dallas in 1963. Amid the grainy footage, chaotic newsreels, and breathless sound bites that comprise our collective memory of that horrible day, Jackie's calm, iconic presence stands out. The image of the stunned widow in her pink wool suit, a copy of a Chanel original, is as familiar to us as that of the black limousine and the grassy knoll. For the next four days, her stoicism in the face of personal tragedy and national crisis would unite the country. Here was her chance to instill a sense of history as the living representative of her husband's presidency, and to leave an indelible impression on a generation. "Jacqueline Kennedy has today given her country the one thing it has always lacked, and that is majesty," a British journalist noted.

For the next twenty-two months, Jackie retreated into mourning. The press and public alike began to look back sentimentally on the Kennedy White House. *Women's Wear Daily*, which was the First Lady's champion and chronicled her styles and trends with great enthusiasm, wrote in April of 1964, "There is no doubt that Mrs. Jacqueline Kennedy probably did more to uplift taste levels in the United States than any woman in the history of our country. And there is no doubt that the entire fashion industry received a major shot in the arm as a result of the constant stream of reports on what Mrs. Kennedy was wearing and where she wore it."

When she emerged from her period of mourning, her style had taken a turn. As a private citizen, no longer confined by official protocol, Jackie embraced a more youthful look, wearing the couture creations of Valentino and Yves Saint Laurent. But her influence had not waned. When she shortened her skirts in the fall of 1966, *The New York Times* announced, "The future of the miniskirt is assured." It was also in 1966 that Jackie was inducted into the International Best-Dressed List Hall of Fame, to honor the profound worldwide impact of her three years in the White House.

Jackie's world shifted dramatically after her departure from the White House in 1963: she wed shipping tycoon Aristotle Onassis, embraced the life of the international jet set, and put aside her Cassini wardrobe in favor of French haute couture.

The social upheaval of the late 1960s was beginning to take its toll on Jackie. The violent death of her husband and then, in 1968, of her brother-in-law Bobby Kennedy, along with the continual attention of the media and public, were wearing her down. Jackie began to loathe her role as a cultural icon and was eager for any change that would break the hold of the Kennedy legacy. When news broke of Jackie's marriage to Greek shipping tycoon Aristotle Onassis, the world was stunned. The two met while she was First Lady; Onassis had offered Jackie the use of his yacht after the death of her infant son, Patrick, in 1963. As Jackie explained to a friend, "Nobody could understand why I married Ari. But I just couldn't live anymore as the Kennedy widow. It was a release, freedom from the oppressive obsession the world has with me."

The wedding created a media blitz. Images of Jackie leaving the chapel with Onassis in her Valentino wedding dress of beige lace and chiffon were flashed around the world. According to Valentino, he immediately received requests from thirty-six brides-to-be for copies of Jackie's wedding dress. By the end of that year, Valentino had sold 150.

With even more money at her disposal than she enjoyed as a Kennedy, Jackie spent extravagantly. She was renowned for her speed-shopping—her ability to spend thousands of dollars in a matter of minutes, buying multiples of anything that caught her eye. She patronized all the great French couturiers: Valentino, Courrèges, Saint Laurent, Madame Grès, Lanvin, Dior, and Givenchy. Each of these designers had at his or her disposal a mannequin with Jackie's measurements: 35-26-38. For years, Jackie had been selling her used clothes at Encore, a consignment shop in Manhattan, in an effort to add to her monthly clothing allowance. She continued to do this after marrying Onassis, consigning coats, suits, gowns, handbags, blouses, and slacks, often after wearing or using them only once.

fter Onassis's death in 1976, Jackie's life was transformed again. Taking another momentous change in stride, Jackie, at the age of forty-seven, became a career woman, signing on as an editor at Viking Press and, later, at Doubleday. During this period, her clothes, while remaining true to her individual style, became more casual and relaxed, with an elegant, businesslike flair. She often wore flowing pants with sweaters or blouses. As part of her transition from jet-setter to career woman, she turned to new sources to help redefine her look. Valentino was replaced with the understated elegance of Carolina Herrera. She left Kenneth Battelle's salon for that of his former employee Thomas Morrissey, who used blonde highlights to lighten Jackie's dark hair to a warm brown.

In Carolina Herrera, Jackie found not only a preferred designer but also a friend. Jackie was completely at ease in Herrera's presence. On one occasion, she happened to be in the designer's showroom trying on clothes when some buyers from Neiman Marcus arrived. As she emerged wearing one of Herrera's suits, Jackie turned to a group of surprised buyers and said, "Don't you think this is lovely?" Herrera also designed the mint-green crepe dress that Jackie wore to the wedding of her daughter, Caroline, in 1986, as well as Caroline's wedding gown. Jackie made a point of staying out of the discussions between the bride-to-be and the designer, sparing her daughter the parental interference she had endured at her own wedding.

Despite the pared-down elegance that characterized her later years, Jackie remained one of the most photographed women in the world. The price of an exclusive photograph of Jackie was rivaled only in years to come by the prices commanded by Diana, Princess of Wales. And Jackie's influence on fashion remained strong. She cleverly camouflaged the signs of aging, and took to wearing white or ivory gloves in public to hide her hands. When photographs of her in gloves began to appear, glove manufacturers were pleasantly surprised to note an upswing in business.

The outpouring of public emotion and the voluminous media coverage that followed Jackie's death in 1994 made it clear that she had retained the love and respect of millions of people. Her legacy was immense. She had redefined the role of First Lady, ensuring that every woman who followed her in the White House would have to carve out her own public image. Her personal style had a tremendous impact that went beyond organizing a knockout wardrobe. For Jackie, style was more than clothes; it was a way of living, a way of imbuing one's life with taste and beauty. Her clothes never overwhelmed her; they were chosen to set off her best features, while remaining comfortable and stylish.

Jackie's importance reaches beyond the trends she created, but she will always be fondly remembered for her influence on American fashion. While there have been other women in our history who have captivated the public imagination, none has possessed the grace, poise, and flair that allowed Jacqueline Kennedy Onassis to create a mystique that spans her generation, those that followed, and those to come.

"Jackie would have preferred to be just herself, but the world insisted that she be a legend too."
—Senator Edward Kennedy

Women
Whit

of the
e House
2

Living in the White House has never been a guarantee of public adulation and acclaim. Indeed, praise has traditionally proven more elusive for first families than for most other public figures. One defining mark of the women featured in this section—Dolley Payne Todd Madison, Julia Gardiner Tyler, Harriet Lane Johnston, Frances Folsom Cleveland Preston, and Alice Roosevelt Longworth—is the extent to which they retained the almost unreserved esteem and love of the nation, often in the midst of political and civil acrimony. In the more than forty presidential administrations that have occupied the White House over the past two centuries, a handful of First Ladies have managed to reshape not only the public perceptions of the nation's executive office but also the underpinnings of our nation's sense of style, fashion, and womanhood.

Soon after the first presidential election in 1789, the American public and press began to wrangle with competing ideas and expectations concerning the role of the President's wife and official White House hostess. From the moment their husbands took office, First Ladies were confronted with the loss of the quiet anonymity that most proper women were expected to treasure and nurture. Then there was the immense challenge of creating a festive, welcoming environment in the politically charged and frequently bellicose city of Washington. From Martha Washington on, presidential wives were inducted, occasionally against their will, into the role both of social leader and standard-bearer of all things fine, elegant, and fashionable. Abigail Adams, the wife of President John Adams, had been a successful hostess in England during her husband's tenure as ambassador to the Court of Saint James. And although her experience abroad served her well as she assumed the duties of the White House, she came to resent the large number of dinners and receptions she was obliged to arrange as First Lady. She also refused to make any changes in her appearance for the sake of fashion. When the artist Gilbert Stuart asked her to pose bareheaded for her portrait, she refused, considering the idea undignified for a fifty-six-year-old woman. Abigail Adams's recalcitrance in the face of her duties stood in sharp contrast to the personality of her successor, Dolley Madison, who delighted in her role. She relished formal entertaining and became a fashion trendsetter by wholeheartedly embracing the daring French gowns that helped chip away at the nation's puritanical foundations.

First Lady Mary Todd Lincoln was certainly aware of Dolley Madison's legacy when she desperately undertook to leave her own mark on the White House. Like Abigail Adams, however, she failed to display the shrewdness and flexibility required to forge an enduring bond with the public. Following the very popular Harriet Lane, Mrs. Lincoln embarked on her career as official hostess by purchasing costly gowns and beginning a long-overdue but expensive redecoration of the White House. In her effort to win recognition and praise, she was oblivious to the dangerous shifts of public opinion, which soon soured on hearing reports of Mrs. Lincoln's lavish expenditures during the brutal deprivations of the Civil War. The flood of reproach deeply and permanently scarred the emotionally fragile First Lady and has continued to haunt her reputation. To this day, the White House under Mary Todd Lincoln remains a dark and misunderstood place.

To trace the history of the role of First Lady, of course, is also to trace the evolution of the American media. The rapid growth of the press in the nineteenth century, and the proliferation of cheap magazines and news-papers targeting a female audience, had by the beginning of the twentieth century trained a virtually unblinking eye on the goings-on in the White House. In an era when women were expected to pay little attention to current events, periodicals instead catered to their female readership by providing lighthearted fashion and society news. Naturally, the women in the White House figured prominently in these columns. The parties they hosted and the clothes they wore were covered in minute detail, and soon the women in the White House, whether they acknowledged it or not, had become role models for generations of women.

In the mid-nineteenth century, when respectable women were expected to keep their names out of the newspaper, First Lady Julia Gardiner Tyler audaciously courted the attention of the media, and complained when she thought the press was delinquent in reporting her activities. By the time Frances Folsom married President Grover Cleveland in 1886, the press had whole corps of reporters assigned to the White House social beat, and prying journalists tracked every move of the newly married couple, even following them on their honeymoon. It would take the cunning and intelligence of Teddy Roosevelt's daughter Alice, some twenty years later, to turn media attention into an advantage for the public image of first families.

Dolley Payne Todd Madison

James Madison became President of the United States nearly two hundred years ago, ushering a fledgling union into the nineteenth century. And yet his wife, Dolley, leaves the more vivid legacy of Madison's tenure in office. Even in our age of modern media scrutiny, when the hairstyles and hemlines of First Ladies are the subjects of daily reports, it is hard to overstate the effect that this woman had on our nation's public image. By all accounts, Dolley was possessed of a wit, a sense of daring, and a physical flair that belied her strict Quaker upbringing. These traits set her apart from her aristocratic detractors and aligned her with the people of a brash, young republic. Dolley Madison's transformation of the White House firmly secured her place in history, and, with the exception of Jacqueline Kennedy, no other First Lady labored so hard to instill an aura of majesty in the executive mansion. She entertained on a lavish scale, greeting her guests in the best French fashions. In the process, Dolley Madison became the first American fashion icon—in effect, the first trendsetter in a young nation coming to terms with its identity.

Captured by the renowned American portraitist Gilbert Stuart in 1804, Dolley Madison was at the threshold of her extraordinary career as Washington's preeminent social doyenne. Pictured at left in the French style of dress she favored, Dolley was the definitive White House hostess.

She was born Dolley Payne on June 20, 1765, at New Garden, a Quaker settlement in North Carolina; soon after her birth, the family moved back to their native Virginia. When she was fifteen, the family moved to Philadelphia to join other Quakers in a more densely populated, urban setting. From an early age, Dolley had a gay personality and a love of beautiful things, predilections that stood in sharp contrast to the somewhat ascetic mores of the Quakers.

In 1790, in accordance with the wishes of her parents and community, Dolley married a fellow Quaker—a lawyer named John Todd—and after two years of marriage their first child, John Payne Todd, was born. The following year Dolley gave birth to another son, William Temple. While Dolley was recovering from the birth of her second child, a yellow fever epidemic struck Philadelphia; panic broke out as the disease spread rapidly through the city. Like many women of her relatively privileged background, Dolley was rushed out of the city with her children, but her husband remained behind to care for his ailing parents, who soon perished. When he finally joined Dolley in the Pennsylvania countryside, he, too, was manifesting symptoms of fever. On October 24, 1793, Dolley's husband and infant son died.

After several months of mourning, the young widow emerged from seclusion, her natural exuberance tested but intact. At twenty-five, Dolley was not conventionally beautiful, but her black hair and creamy complexion set her apart from other women. "She has a fine person and most engaging countenance, which pleases, not so much from mere symmetry or complexion, as from expression," one congressman of the era remarked. "Her smile, her conversation, and her manners are so engaging, that it is no wonder that such a young widow, with her fine blue eyes and large share of animation, should be indeed, a Queen of Hearts."

After Dolley's father died in 1792, her mother turned the family home into a boarding house for politicians serving in the new federal government—among them a lawyer and congressman from New York, Aaron Burr. He represented Dolley in a legal suit over her late husband's estate. As the nation's first capital, Philadelphia was a bustling city filled with interesting and powerful men. And Dolley, though recently widowed, charmed and attracted suitors. One evening she sent a frantic note to a friend: "Thou must come to me. Aaron Burr says that the great little Madison has asked to [see] me this evening."

James Madison, by the age of forty-three, had made quite a career for himself in politics. A student of political history and law, he was regarded as the Father of the Constitution for his brilliant work in drafting the laws of the United States and his leading role at the Constitutional Convention. Only five feet four inches tall and weighing barely one hundred pounds, Madison was often mocked for his small stature as well as for the dour expression he wore in public. In the company of friends, however, he was charming and witty. Having seen Dolley about town, Madison, then majority leader in the House of Representatives, persuaded Burr, his former Princeton University classmate, to arrange a formal introduction. At their first meeting, Madison was, by all accounts, completely captivated.

hospitality, and even receiving compliments from that old curmudgeon, Vice President John Adams. Living in what was then considered one of the most elegant cities in the country, Dolley soon developed a taste for the finest French clothes and furnishings. Many of her purchases were made through American diplomats, especially James Monroe, who, on behalf of the Madisons, chose from the auction houses of Paris an assortment of furnishings formerly belonging to the ill-fated French aristocracy.

Although seventeen years Dolley's senior, he asked her to marry him after a brief courtship. His proposal posed a moral dilemma for the recently widowed Dolley: marriage to the non-Quaker Madison would mean exclusion from the Quaker community. After months of persistence, however, James Madison persuaded Dolley Todd to wed, and they were married on September 15, 1794.

Dolley and James Madison set up housekeeping in a large house in the center of Philadelphia. While her marriage excluded her from the world in which she had been raised, it introduced her to one filled with new possibilities. Freed from Quaker restrictions, Dolley began to embrace those facets of life that she had previously been prevented from enjoying. As the wife of one of the leaders of the Republican Party, she was responsible for entertaining statesmen and foreign dignitaries on a regular basis. She apparently had no trouble making the transition from Quaker widow to politician's wife, winning praise from her guests for her generous

In June of 1800, the federal government was moved from Philadelphia to Washington. Later that year, when Thomas Jefferson was elected president, he appointed as secretary of state his close friend and protégé James Madison, thus affording Dolley her earliest glimpses of the presidential quarters. Within two months of his inauguration, President Jefferson, a widower, began to call on Dolley to act as White House hostess in the absence of a First Lady. Dolley relished this role and the opportunity to participate in the highest level of political life. She made great use of social gatherings to further her husband's political objectives; enemies were persuaded to put aside their antagonisms, and Dolley was able to glean politically valuable information from guests in a friendly, unobtrusive manner. Her great diplomatic skill and personal warmth made many friends for her husband, and her soirees were the toast of Washington. Colonel André de Bronne, a French military attaché, noted, "Mrs. Madison has become one of America's most valuable assets."

As wife of the secretary of state, Dolley was in contact with a host of foreign dignitaries. She became acquainted with the wife of the French foreign minister, Madame Pichon, who introduced Dolley to the latest French fashions. "[Madame Pichon] shows me everything she has and would fain give of me everything. She decorates herself according to the French ideas and wishes me to do so too," Mrs. Madison wrote to her sister in 1804. By the time Napoleon seized power in 1799, Paris reigned as the fashion capital of the world, following the elegant example set by the first consul's stylish wife, Josephine. By the early 1800s, as the rhetoric of piety and self-reliance stirred up by the American Revolution began to soften, women in this country were becoming less reluctant to look to Europe for inspiration in their modes of dress and decorum. For a new republic with no indigenous fashion to speak of, Paris was an invisible beacon of all things elegant and stylish. But the French style, while irresistible and wildly popular, posed problems in a social landscape rooted more in Calvinism than in the warm humanism of the Enlightenment. For many Americans, this fashion, which consisted of fine, sheer fabrics, high waists, low necklines, and short sleeves, denoted a lack of modesty. While American

women were intrigued by the new slim silhouette, deference to prevailing American standards led them to wear the skirts of their gowns a little fuller and their necklines a little higher. Soon, however, Dolley became the greatest and most visible proponent of the French style, and her mode of dress immediately stirred controversy.

Dolley was vastly popular, but like so many newcomers to the social elite, she had her detractors. Mrs. Merry, wife of the English ambassador Anthony Merry, was fond of criticizing what she deemed the provincial trappings of Dolley's parties, complaining that the food was "more like a harvest home supper than the entertainment of a Secretary of State." Dolley's unabashed response is a wonderful example of the diplomatic put-down: "But abundance is preferable to elegance . . . The profusion so repugnant to foreign customs rises from the happy circumstances of the abundance and prosperity of our country. I don't hesitate to sacrifice the delicacy of European taste for the less elegant, but more liberal fashion of Virginia." Dolley's remarkable combination of feistiness and diplomacy would serve her well in the years that followed, as all eyes turned to her husband's political ascension.

Typical Quaker dress, as shown here on this eighteenth-century painted tray, stood in sharp contrast to the comparatively revealing fashions worn by most people of that era. At one White House dinner, the controversial nature of the First Lady's mode of dress was clearly apparent. Dolley toasted a fellow Quaker: "Here's to thy absent broad-brim, Friend Hallowell"—a reference to the fact that her guest was not wearing his usual Quaker hat. Mr. Hallowell responded, "And here's to thy absent kerchief, Friend Dorothy," referring to the lack of coverage the French dress afforded Mrs. Madison's bosom.

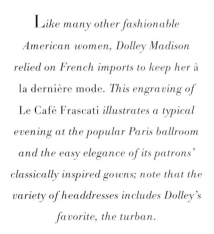

Like many other fashionable American women, Dolley Madison relied on French imports to keep her à la dernière mode. This engraving of Le Café Frascati *illustrates a typical evening at the popular Paris ballroom and the easy elegance of its patrons' classically inspired gowns; note that the variety of headdresses includes Dolley's favorite, the turban.*

Following the precedent set by George Washington, Thomas Jefferson declined to run for a third term, and after eight years as secretary of state, James Madison was elected in 1808 as the fourth President of the United States, winning an easy victory. On March 4, 1809, a formal inaugural ceremony took place in Washington. After being sworn in, the new President, accompanied by the newly dubbed Lady Presidentess, hosted an afternoon reception to greet their well-wishers. Dolley wore a plain cambric dress with a low neckline and a very long train, along with a bonnet of purple velvet and white satin embellished by white plumes. She was a portrait of simple elegance, embodying a unique fusion of American straightforwardness and European sophistication.

That evening, more than four hundred people crowded into a Washington hotel for the inaugural ball. Among those attending was Margaret Bayard Smith, wife of the founder of the country's first national newspaper,

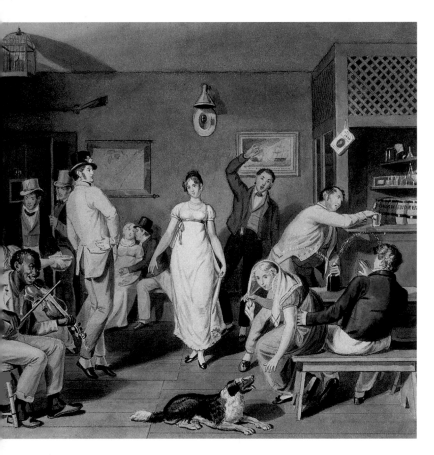

At a country party, as in the John Louis Krimmel painting Barroom Dancing (left), or an evening soiree, as in Henry Sargent's The Tea Party (right), American women emulated the fashions of the popular First Lady. Dolley Madison's celebrated "drawing rooms" might have resembled the elegant scene at right.

the *Intelligencer*. "Poor Mrs. Madison was almost pressed to death," Mrs. Smith recounted, "for every one crowded round her . . . to have a peep of her. She looked a queen. She had on a pale buff colored velvet, made plain, with a very long train, but not the least trimming, and [a] beautiful pearl necklace, earrings and bracelets. Her headdress was a turban of the same colored velvet and white satin (from Paris) with two superb plumes, the bird of paradise feathers. [She possesses] unassuming dignity, sweetness and grace. She really, in manners and appearance, answered all my ideas of royalty."

Though she did indeed dress like a queen, Dolley's easygoing manner made her the embodiment of the republican woman.

Dolley was as determined as her husband to ensure that his presidency be a brilliant success. She recognized that Jefferson's administration, though politically enlightened, had failed to inject a sense of majesty and power into the office of the President. Dolley began her efforts with the White House itself. Ever since John and Abigail Adams had moved into the unfinished mansion

in 1800, no attempt had been made to properly furnish its rooms and grounds. Congress appropriated the necessary funds, and with the guidance of architect Benjamin Latrobe, who designed the Capitol building, Dolley decorated the White House in harmony with many of the other buildings of the new capital—in the neoclassical style widely accepted as the most fitting for a nation whose democratic ideals could be traced to the civilizations of ancient Greece and Rome. Inspired by a profusion of Greek artifacts recently unearthed by archaeologists, designers like Latrobe fully embraced this neoclassical vision of American style. Indeed, Latrobe's designs for chairs (below) and sofas, which were executed by a Baltimore firm, borrowed heavily from ancient Greek prototypes. His versions featured splayed legs and curved backs, but, unlike the ancient originals, were painted and gilded, with cane seats softened by the addition of velvet cushions. Dolley's oval drawing room, where company was received, was furnished with chairs

and sofas upholstered in yellow damask with matching drapery. The centerpiece of the room was a decorative rising-sun motif that hung above the mantel and was made from the same yellow fabric. Dolley would position herself before the mantel, her back to the rising sun, to greet her guests. Aside from Jacqueline Kennedy Onassis, no other First Lady exhibited so much care and dedication in transforming the White House into a symbol of presidential prestige.

Once the redecoration was complete, Dolley opened the White House to the public. Every Wednesday evening

Opposite: *The Tea Party*, Henry Sargent, ca. 1824. Gift of Mrs. Horatio A. Lamb in memory of Mr. and Mrs. Winthrop Sargent. Courtesy of Museum of Fine Arts, Boston.

she hosted social gatherings known as "drawing rooms," after the venue in which they were commonly held. No invitation was needed, and people from any walk of life could attend, as long as they were suitably dressed. These weekly affairs were nicknamed "Mrs. Madison's squeezes"—sometimes as many as three hundred people would cram themselves into the relatively small, formal rooms. The drawing rooms became a forum for people to discuss politics or seek political appointments. Others came to flirt, to meet an eligible mate, or simply to show off their stylish clothes. The writer Washington Irving, who attended several Wednesday night drawing rooms, wrote, "Mrs. Madison is a fine, portly, buxom dame, who has a smile and a pleasant word for everybody." Dolley Madison had rapidly become the center of Washington's social universe.

Dolley may have been a republican at heart, but she did not hesitate to defer to Europe in all matters of fashion and taste. She relied on friends and politicians in France to provide her with clothes and accessories. To Mr. and Mrs. Joel Barlow, the American minister to France and his wife, she wrote in 1811, "As you, my dear friends, have everything and we nothing that is beautiful, I will ask the favor of you to send me by a safe vessel large headdresses, a few flowers, feathers, gloves and stockings, black and white, with anything else pretty." One of her overseas shipments cost more than two thousand dollars in duties alone. Dolley was especially fond of her elaborate turbans, which were a hallmark of her evening ensembles and reportedly cost as much as one thousand dollars a year.

The First Lady's devotion to fine clothes and parties, combined with her high visibility, soon made her the primary source of fashion trends for American women. Her clothes permeated the public consciousness, and detailed descriptions of them appear constantly in the diaries, letters, and newspapers of the period. The following examples give a sense of Dolley's elaborate wardrobe:

The First Lady wore a white cambric dress, buttoned all the way up and with a strip of embroidery along the buttonholes and a ruffled hem. [Over her] shoulder [was] a peach-colored silk scarf with a rich border. Her satin spencer was the same color, also her gauze turban.

[She] wore her finest jewels . . . her gown [of] yellow satin [was] embroidered all over with sprigs of butterflies, her bonnet a feathered creation.

[Dolley] startled everyone by wearing black velvet, gold trimmed and worn with a gold lace turban, with a tiara with twenty-three sapphires. She looked brilliant.

Mrs. Madison appeared in a toilet of rose-colored satin [with a] white velvet train, which swept the floor for several yards. The train was lined with lavender satin and edged with a ruching of lace. She wore a gold girdle and gold necklace and bracelets. This costume was completed by a turban of white velvet, trimmed with white ostrich tips, and a gold embroidered crown.

During her husband's 1808 presidential campaign, the newspapers printed wild rumors accusing Dolley of being Thomas Jefferson's mistress. This bad press, instigated by her husband's radical political opponents, taught her the importance of the media's role in maintaining a favorable public image. Dolley became more shrewd in her socializing and formed close friendships with Margaret Bayard Smith and Sarah Gales Seaton, whose husband was coeditor of the *Intelligencer*. Thanks to the influence of these women, stories of Dolley's wit, fashions, and social gatherings continued to circulate throughout the country, offsetting the negative effect of the earlier reports. In 1818, she became the first wife of a President to be featured on the cover of a magazine when *Portfolio*, a Philadelphia-based publication, had an engraving made from one of her portraits.

Dolley Madison's power as a female public figure in this country was unprecedented. An author looking for her support wrote, "The elevation of your Rank, together with . . . your spirit . . . gives you an Influence which no other lady can pretend to, especially among the Fair Sex of our Country . . . I had rather have a few lines from Mrs. Madison than from a whole Bunch of Bishops." Dolley used her influence to raise the prestige of women, encouraging them to attend debates in Congress and observe the oral arguments presented to the Supreme Court. When she encouraged others to join her in sponsoring the Washington City Orphan Asylum, it was the first time the wife of a President publicly championed a social cause.

Even after Dolley and President Madison had retired to their Virginia home, Dolley maintained the fashion precedent she had set, as evidenced by this fabric from an exquisitely embroidered satin gown.

Madisons lived in other homes in Washington.

It was with much regret that, in 1816, Dolley left Washington for Montpelier, the Madison family home in Virginia. After sixteen years as the nation's hostess, she had become accustomed to the excitement associated with her position. But despite Montpelier's country setting, Dolley continued to entertain on a lavish scale. Harriet Martineau, the English writer and economist, visited Dolley in Montpelier twenty years after the Madisons' retirement from politics. She remarked that Dolley was still "celebrated throughout the country for the grace and dignity with which she discharged the arduous duties which revolve upon the President's lady. For a term of eight years, she dispensed the hospitalities of the White House with such discretion, impartiality and kindness, that it is believed that she gratified everyone and offended nobody."

Feeling out of touch at her plantation home, Dolley wrote her niece in 1826 for the latest fashion news: "We are very old-fashioned here. Can you send me a paper pattern of the present sleeve, and describe the width of dress and waist; also how turbans are pinned up, bonnets worn, as well as how to behave in the fashion?"

James Madison won the election of 1812, and as he began his second term, war with Britain was imminent. In an effort to boost the nation's morale, Dolley kept up a hectic social schedule, and continued to organize events even as residents of Washington fled the approaching British army. While her husband accompanied troops in the field, Dolley remained alone in the White House, packing up government papers, including the Constitution and the Declaration of Independence, which she sent ahead with some of her personal possessions for safekeeping. They survive today thanks to her efforts. She remained in the White House until the last possible moment, refusing to leave until the large Gilbert Stuart portrait of George Washington had been taken down and removed from the city. Dolley's courage in the face of danger (the British commander had bragged he would kidnap Dolley and parade her through the streets of London) made her a national hero. When the British set fire to Washington, the White House—the scene of so many triumphs for Dolley—was virtually destroyed. For the remaining two years of the presidential term, the

After her husband's death in 1836, Dolley returned to the capital, becoming the grande dame of Washington society. But she was by then a lady of greatly reduced means. Her only surviving child—her son, Payne, from her first marriage—squandered his mother's money and his stepfather's estate, leaving Dolley nearly destitute. After Dolley made repeated offers, the government agreed to purchase her husband's private papers; she eventually sold them in two installments totaling $55,000, though they were reported to be worth $100,000.

Despite her financial worries, Dolley relished life in Washington. Her successors in the White House treated her with deference, often turning to her for advice; the traditional New Year's and Independence Day social calls on the White House were invariably followed by a trip to Dolley's Washington home. There, guests took pleasure in seeing Mrs. Madison still dressed in the gowns and turbans from her White House years, though they were by that time quite out of fashion. Most visitors remarked that they liked seeing her just as she had appeared in her glory days.

Even in old age, Dolley Madison was unequivocally one of the best-known and most-loved women in America. In 1844, Congress invited her to sit among its members, rather than in the public gallery, whenever she visited. This was perhaps the greatest honor ever received by an American woman of that era, when female lawmakers, not to mention female voters, were unheard of. In her mid-seventies, she never turned down an invitation to a party, admitting to a niece, "You know, I usually like the routs [parties] too well." At age seventy-six, she became the second person in history to send a message via Morse code (Samuel Morse was the first). Four years later, she stood on the dais as the cornerstone was laid for the Washington Monument. Shortly before her death, Dolley attended the farewell reception for President Polk, wearing a new gown made especially for the event. The white satin gown with deep décolletage and short sleeves, worn with a feathered turban trimmed in fringe, was familiar to all as Dolley's trademark style, and the guests were surprised to see that at eighty, Dolley was a little plumper, but that her skin retained its youthful glow.

Dolley Madison died in her sleep on July 12, 1849. Hundreds of people lined up to see her lying in state at Saint John's Church in Washington (she had embraced her husband's Episcopalian faith). Every department in the federal government sent a representative to Dolley's funeral, and the funeral procession was at the time the largest ever to march through the city. The President himself, Zachary Taylor, eulogized her: "She will never be forgotten, because she was truly our First Lady for a half-century." Although this was the first recorded usage of this term, the label was not commonly accepted until the presidency of James Buchanan, when it was applied to his niece and official hostess, Harriet Lane.

In the early twentieth century, during a resurgence of interest in American history, a sort of Dolley Madison revival took place. A comedy about her life, *First Lady of the Land*, appeared on Broadway in 1911, and the following year Congressional wives hosted a birthday brunch in her honor. That event sparked a renewed interest in all First Ladies and is credited with inspiring the idea for the collection of inaugural gowns that is now on display at the Smithsonian Institution. Until well into this century, Dolley Madison remained the standard by which all First Ladies were judged.

A silhouette of Dolley from around 1785–90 (above) was completed before her first marriage, to fellow Quaker John Todd. In an 1817 portrait by Bass Otis (right), Dolley sports her usual décolletage and turban. This image was reproduced on the cover of Philadelphia's Portfolio *magazine, making Dolley the first President's wife to be so featured, and inaugurating a marketing trend: the selling of the First Lady to the American public.*

Julia Gardiner Tyler

Julia Tyler presented this 1848 portrait by Francesco Anelli to the White House in 1869. Julia, wearing a diamond ferronière in her hair, embodied youth and vivacity, and looked every bit the New York society belle who captivated Washington politicians and won the heart of a President.

A fiercely independent, if pious, republican sentiment had defined the early years of nineteenth-century America. But, by the mid-1800s, it was superseded by the values of the Victorian era. Victorian social wisdom held that women should be firmly rooted in the domestic sphere, maintaining a constant, tight-lipped decorum. It was in this calcified era that Julia Gardiner Tyler came of age and—perhaps in defiance of the stifling moral climate—actively sought out the adulation and attention she craved. She was only nineteen in 1839 when she violated an unwritten code of modesty by agreeing to appear in an advertisement for a New York City department store. With a knack for self-promotion worthy of an aspiring Hollywood actor, Julia became a local celebrity overnight. She drew the national gaze again in 1844, when she became the first woman to marry a sitting President, and became John Tyler's wife.

Born into one of New York's oldest and wealthiest families, Julia was already accustomed to luxuries that most women in preindustrial America never enjoyed; her affluent background fueled her lifelong passion for beautiful clothes and handsome furnishings. But it was more than upper-class tastes that allowed Julia, during the brief nine months she inhabited the White House, to create a vibrant social world that would be remembered for years to come. And while she cannot be credited with the popularization of any one fashion trend, the attention the media showered on her made her one of the most visible women in the country. She became a cultural icon for a generation of women during an era when few garnered national attention.

Julia Gardiner was born in 1820 to David Gardiner—a New York state senator from a wealthy and socially prominent family who owned Gardiner's Island, off the tip of Long Island—and Juliana McLachlan, the daughter of a prosperous New York City brewer of Scottish descent. Her mother had a domineering personality and controlled the lives of all her children—with the exception of Julia. While attending the fashionable Madame N. D. Chagaray's Institute on Houston Street in New York, Julia regularly received letters from her mother. In her habitually elitist tone, Juliana insisted that her daughter be one of the best-dressed young women in New York. "You must not be so much afraid of being extravagant," she urged. "You must recollect that it requires considerable money to be fashionable in the city and I wish you to appear in a manner that will be agreeable." While Julia may have bristled in typical teenage fashion at her mother's advice, she nevertheless took it quite to heart.

When Julia was fifteen, she made her official society debut, wearing one of her mother's best formal gowns, pearl earrings, and a bouquet of flowers at her bosom. After graduating from Madame Chagaray's in 1838, Julia returned to her family's home in rural East Hampton, Long Island. She missed the excitement of living in New York, and frequently wrote to her brother Alexander, asking for the latest gossip and including with her letters detailed shopping lists for dress fabrics and accessories. From the outset, Julia exercised a strong will and an assertive sense of personal style. On one occasion, after receiving what she deemed an unsatisfactory shipment from New York, she wrote to her brother, "I intend

This lithograph depicts Julia, dressed fashionably in a fur-trimmed coat with a feathered bonnet, carrying a large handbag that announces, "I'll Purchase at Bogart & Mecamly's No. 86, 9th Ave. Their Goods are Beautiful & Astonishingly Cheap." Below this image was printed Julia's well-known emblem, the Rose of Long Island.

returning you those exquisite pink gloves for you to change . . . I think Taste hid herself in your pocket when they were selected."

Julia may have been looking for a little excitement when, in 1839, she secretly agreed to pose for an advertising handbill for a low-end Manhattan clothing store. Her family and high-society peers were shocked. No woman of social standing had ever permitted the exploitation of her image in the name of a commercial enterprise (much less in an endorsement of inexpensive clothes)—a move that dangerously straddled the all-important divide between the social elite and the public at large. Several months later, in May of 1840, another scandal broke when a poem dedicated to "Julia—The Rose of Long Island" appeared on the front page of the *Brooklyn Daily News*. Julia relished the public attention but had once again allowed the hermetic world of the New York aristocracy to be penetrated. This was the last straw for David and Juliana Gardiner. In September of 1840, the Gardiners took Julia and her sister Margaret on a year-long tour of Europe.

Julia flirted and danced her way across the Continent. In England, Lydia Sigourney, the popular American author, took note of the stir created by this American newcomer: "English beaux on meeting her seemed suddenly to become aware of the value of their lost colonies." In France, she was presented at the court of Louis Philippe and was overwhelmed by its opulence and pageantry. While abroad, Julia read with increasing interest press accounts concerning President Martin Van Buren's daughter-in-law Angelica, who was said to be fond of copying the royal protocol of the courts of Europe when presiding over White House functions.

In January of 1842, the Gardiners left Europe to spend the winter season in Washington. Within weeks, they were invited to the White House by the son of Van Buren's successor, President John Tyler. There, Julia Gardiner, then a twenty-two-year-old society belle, met the fifty-two-year-old then-married President of the United States. John Tyler had been the first Vice President to assume the duties of the presidency, after William Henry Harrison died of pneumonia one month following his inauguration. An independent thinker, Tyler received constant criticism from both political parties, but was a warm and gracious host at White House social events and was known for his easy charm.

When the Gardiners returned to Washington in December of that year for the start of the Washington social season, the nation's capital was in mourning. Letitia Tyler, the President's wife, had died in September, and the Gardiners were among those friends of the first family invited to the White House to comfort the President. Despite the city's muted atmosphere, Julia continued to take Washington society by storm. *The New York Herald* reported, "The beautiful and accomplished Miss Gardner [sic] of Long Island, one of the loveliest women in the United States, is in the city [Washington], and was the 'observed of all observers' during her promenade on the avenue today."

Julia Gardiner was admired by both American society and the courts of Europe as a great beauty. She was small, about five feet three inches tall, with dark, nearly black, hair, which she wore parted down the middle and

*P*olitically beleaguered President John Tyler paid twenty-two-year-old Julia Gardiner "a thousand compliments" at their first meeting in 1842.

close to her head. She had large, dark, oval eyes, full lips, and a curvaceous figure (she frequently complained about her weight). Coupled with Julia's striking looks were a vitality and a genuine passion for living. Nineteenth-century historian Elizabeth Ellet commented that Julia was "sparkling and attractive, without affectation; she had a high and daring spirit." As the toast of Washington, she flirted with men her own age as well as with those older than her father, including future President James Buchanan and various members of the Supreme Court. Her arrival in the visitors' gallery above the House or Senate floors typically caused a substantial commotion, as senators and representatives actually left the floor to dote upon her.

Julia's charms were not lost on President Tyler. Lonely after his wife's death, he quickly became enthralled with this vivacious young woman and began to court her—to the extent that decency allowed for a widower of five months. By February of 1843, John Tyler was, by all accounts, deeply in love. On the night of the Washington's Birthday ball at the White House, Tyler took Julia aside and proposed. She initially declined. On that particular evening, Julia wore a white tarlatan gown and a crimson Greek hat with a dangling tassel, and at one point during their encounter, she later recalled, she shook her head so vigorously in response to the President's pleas that the tassel of her hat hit Tyler square in the face. "It was undignified, but it amused me very much to see his expression as he tried to make love to me and the tassel brushed his face." But by the time the social season came to an end in March, Julia had capitulated and entered into a secret engagement with the President. Only twenty-three years old, Julia would be the first woman to marry a sitting

President as well as the second-youngest woman ever to serve as First Lady. Her youth made her somewhat of a novelty, and the media would focus their considerable attention on the publicity-conscious Julia, who was soon to become the best-known and most-recognized woman in the country.

Currier and Ives took artistic license in their recreation of the tragic explosion that killed Julia's father, David Gardiner. Here, Julia is erroneously placed beside the mast of the naval ship Princeton; *in fact, she was below deck when the accident occurred.*

John Tyler didn't see Julia again until she returned to Washington with her father and sister on February 24, 1844. A few days later, the Gardiners joined the President and more than 350 guests (among them Dolley Madison) for an excursion along the Potomac on the navy ship *Princeton* to observe the firing of the world's largest naval gun, the Peacemaker. During an encore performance near Mount Vernon, the cannon exploded, sending chunks of jagged hot iron flying across the deck and blowing away a twenty-foot section of the hull. Eight people were killed in the explosion, including David Gardiner. Informed of

her father's death, Julia fainted and was carried across a gangplank to another ship by President Tyler. The Gardiner sisters stayed at the White House while preparations were made to provide for a state funeral, after which the Gardiner family returned to East Hampton.

John Tyler was kind and supportive to Julia and her family after David Gardiner's death. In her grief, Julia drew closer to the President, and, within weeks, decided that expediting her marriage to Tyler would help her overcome her sorrow. "After I lost my father I felt differently toward the President," Julia wrote. "He seemed to fill the place and to be more agreeable in every way than any younger man ever was or could be."

On April 20, 1844, seven weeks after David Gardiner's death, John Tyler wrote Julia's mother requesting permission to marry her daughter. Ever the class-conscious patrician, Juliana Gardiner, while fond of the President, initially questioned whether a Virginia planter—President or not—could afford to provide adequately for her daughter. "Julia in her tastes and inclinations is neither extravagant nor unreasonable tho' she has been accustomed to all the necessary comforts and elegancies of life," she responded to the President's letter. Despite her concerns for her daughter's financial future, Juliana ultimately gave her blessing.

Late in the evening of June 25, 1844, President John Tyler arrived in New York City and slipped into Howard's Hotel, at the corner of Broadway and Maiden Lane; the hotel staff was not allowed to leave the premises for fear they would leak news that the President was in town. The next day, John Tyler was wed to Julia Gardiner by the bishop of New York in a small service at the Episcopal Church of the Ascension, at Fifth Avenue and Tenth Street. The bride set aside her mourning clothes for the occasion, wearing a simple white dress of *lisse* and a wreath of white flowers in her hair. (White wedding gowns were still something of a novelty at the time; it had been only four years since the twenty-one-year-old Queen Victoria had donned a white bridal gown, giving rise to a steady tide of imitators.) While Julia's gown does not appear to have survived, it would have followed the era's prevailing style, which featured a long, lean silhouette. Bodices, although still worn over a corset, were boned and elongated through dropped, pointed waistlines; sleeves were tight and narrow; necklines were conservative, even for evening wear; and skirts were dome-shaped, with hems that brushed the floor.

After the ceremony, the guests returned to the Gardiners' New York home on Lafayette Place. Later that day, Julia changed into a black traveling gown and departed with the President for Washington. When news of the wedding broke, the press was furious to discover they had been excluded. New York and Washington society and the public at large, on the other hand, were amused to hear that the President had "eloped" with a woman younger than three of his daughters. Some journalists found the situation especially humorous and printed sly observations about the President's ability to perform his "official duties."

Public reaction to Julia was mixed. *The New York Herald* praised her as "one of the most accomplished daughters of the State of New York" and added that "all proper measures [should be] taken to ensure the reign of so much loveliness for four years longer in the White House." Still, the loudest voices were those of censure, sometimes bordering on abuse. New York attorney George Templeton Strong recorded the following thoughts on the matter in his diary: "I've just heard a rumor that infatuated old John Tyler was married today to one of these large, fleshy Miss Gardiners of Gardiners Island. Poor, unfortunate, deluded old jackass."

Despite the ribald jokes and public reprobation, Julia thoroughly enjoyed being thrust into the limelight. On her journey to Washington, she wrote to her mother, "Wherever we stopped, wherever we went, crowds of people, outstripping one another, came to gaze at the President's bride . . . the secrecy of the affair is on the tongue and admiration of everyone. Everyone says it was the best managed thing they ever heard of. The President says I am the best of diplomats." After the couple's arrival at the White House on June 28, a large wedding reception was held; Dolley Madison, with whom Julia immediately sensed a natural affinity, was one of the guests. Realizing they shared a passion for socializing, and aware of Dolley's experience in that field, Julia often sought Dolley's advice, frequently inviting her to the White House.

Embracing her new role as First Lady, Julia basked in the attention lavished upon her. Unabashed as always, she wrote her mother, "I have commenced my auspicious reign and am in quiet possession of the Presidential Mansion . . . This winter I intend to do something in the way of entertaining that shall be the admiration and talk of all the Washington world." In preparation for the coming social season, which would begin when Congress resumed in December, Julia set about putting the White House in order. As a result of the continual opposition the President faced in Congress, money had not been appropriated for the upkeep of the White House—not even for basic housekeeping. Julia's mother stepped in, financing a minor refurbishment to make the mansion more suitable for entertaining and more livable for the first family.

A distinctive characteristic of evening dress in the 1840s was the flounced skirt, as seen in the fashion plate at right. Julia wore a similar gown of embroidered white gauze (see detail below) at her presentation to the court of King Louis Philippe of France in 1840. In 1937, the gown (above) was included in a paper-doll book featuring dresses worn by America's First Ladies from the collection of the Smithsonian Institution.

imply put, Julia interpreted the role of First Lady as that of a queen. Having visited the court of Louis Philippe of France during her year abroad in 1840, Julia used it as a model for White House protocol in an effort to instill some of the pomp and grandeur of royalty into the American presidency. She instructed the Marine Band to play "Hail to the Chief" every time the President entered the room. She created a "court" composed of young female members of the Gardiner and Tyler families who served as her ladies-in-waiting. These women, whom Julia's detractors referred to as "the vestal virgins," numbered anywhere from six to twelve. Wearing matching white gowns, they stood behind Julia at social events in two angled columns, while the First Lady seated herself on a raised platform and nodded to her guests. Evening attire in the 1840s was not very different from day dresses of the period, except that necklines, which were worn off the shoulder, were more revealing, and sleeves were short and tight. Fabrics for evening tended to be either light cottons, such as organdy, which were worn as flounced skirts, or heavier fabrics, such as silks and satins, which were often embellished with lace or other decorative trims. Wherever Julia went, including parties outside the White House, her "court" followed behind.

As extravagant as her monarchical pretensions may have seemed, Julia knew she needed a positive public image and was shrewd enough to recognize the role of the press in fostering it. She befriended the bachelor F. W. Thomas, a correspondent for *The New York Herald*, who served as her de facto press agent during her tenure in the White House. He heaped praise on Julia, singling out her many graces and the triumphs of her social events. On one occasion, he wrote a flattering piece that compared Julia to Queen Victoria, who was a year older than the First Lady. He claimed that Julia was "far more beautiful, younger, more intelligent, and Republican than the Queen, and as popular with the general public as Her Majesty." Thomas fell from favor only when he was slow to submit articles on the First Lady and when, in a risky lapse of judgment, he described her in one article as "rosy and fat."

As she was still in mourning for her father, Julia wore black dresses during the day and white gowns for evening. Her spirited fashion sense was hardly dampened, however, and she continued to send letters to her family in New York, requesting fashionable materials that included, in one memorable case, "something pretty in the way of mourning silks." Her most frequent complaint to her family was that Washington's notorious heat waves often caused the dyes of her black gowns to bleed, staining her neck and arms.

Julia's evening gowns were exquisite. She labored over her appearance, carefully gauging the impact it would have on her guests. The effect, by all accounts, was magical, especially upon those visiting from the country's more provincial western states. Julia's New York shopping lists outlined in detail her wardrobe plans: "I intend to have a sort of velvet cap with a Heron's plume in front pinned on with my large diamond pin." She also frequently wore a diamond *ferronière* for evening events. The *ferronière*, inspired by an ornament popular during the Italian Renaissance, consisted of a band worn around the head, typically featuring a decorative element, such as a precious stone, at the center of the brow. Leonardo da Vinci's portrait of the Virgin Mary shows the Virgin wearing a similar accessory.

Julia's ensembles and parties began to generate substantial attention. At one White House ball, she was described as looking "stunning in black embroidered lace over white satin, set off with black and silver trim, and [with a set of diamonds]." After one of Julia's soirees, her sister Margaret wrote, "She was wearing a new white satin dress overlaid with white lace, a white satin headdress with three white ostrich feathers, and her set of diamonds."

Julia's White House parties were copied throughout Washington—even when they strayed from accepted protocol, as when the First Lady shocked society by introducing the polka and the waltz at one of her galas. With Mrs. Tyler's tacit seal of approval, the dances spread throughout the country—one composer even dedicated a suite of waltzes to her.

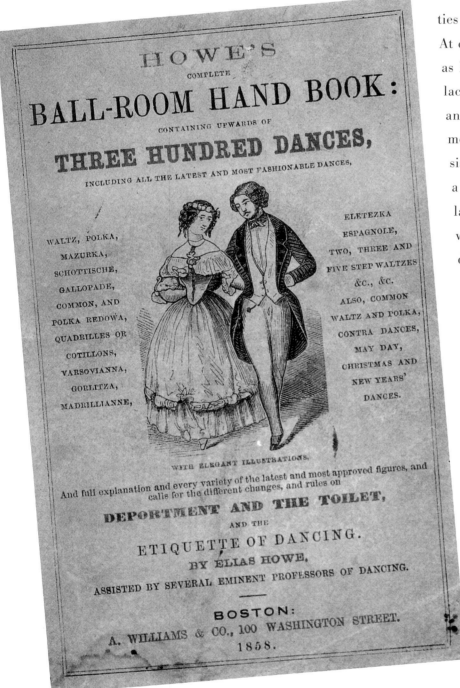

HOWE'S
COMPLETE
BALL-ROOM HAND BOOK:
CONTAINING UPWARDS OF
THREE HUNDRED DANCES,
INCLUDING ALL THE LATEST AND MOST FASHIONABLE DANCES,

WALTZ, POLKA, MAZURKA, SCHOTTISCHE, GALLOPADE, COMMON, AND POLKA REDOWA, QUADRILLES OR COTILLONS, VARSOVIANNA, GORLITZA, MADRILLIANNE,

ELETEZKA ESPAGNOLE, TWO, THREE AND FIVE STEP WALTZES &c., &c. ALSO, COMMON WALTZ AND POLKA, CONTRA DANCES, MAY DAY, CHRISTMAS AND NEW YEARS' DANCES.

WITH ELEGANT ILLUSTRATIONS,
And full explanation and every variety of the latest and most approved figures, and calls for the different changes, and rules on
DEPORTMENT AND THE TOILET,
AND THE
ETIQUETTE OF DANCING.
BY ELIAS HOWE,
ASSISTED BY SEVERAL EMINENT PROFESSORS OF DANCING.

BOSTON:
A. WILLIAMS & CO., 100 WASHINGTON STREET.
1858.

Julia's parties were not merely idle entertainments. A "born ballroom lobbyist," she used social events to help shore up support for key issues of her husband's political agenda, in particular the annexation of Texas. When Texas finally agreed to join the Union in 1845, the success was seen as one shared by the President and the First Lady. John Tyler gave his wife the gold pen he used to sign the proclamation, and with tremendous pride she wore it as a pendant on a gold chain.

Toward the end of his first term as President, John Tyler was besieged on all sides by the leading political parties of his day, and he decided not to run for a second term. But Julia was determined to conclude her tenure at the White House with a flourish. The Tylers hosted a farewell ball on February 18, 1845, attended by an estimated three thousand guests—a thousand more than had been invited. More than six hundred candles illuminated the White House that evening as guests consumed cases of champagne and barrels of wine. Julia wore an exquisite gown of white satin embroidered with silver and trimmed with white roses, a silver-embroidered white satin headdress trimmed with three ostrich feathers, and her ubiquitous set of diamonds. In the face of a waning presidency and a fractured political scene, Julia Gardiner Tyler managed to stage what was possibly the most exuberant and lavish social event ever hosted at the executive mansion. Afterward, Julia's sister Margaret wrote with pride, "All acknowledge that nothing half so grand had been seen at the White House during any Administration, and fear nothing so tasteful would be again." Thanks to press articles written by F. W. Thomas and Julia's brother, the party received national attention and assured that Julia would leave a lasting impression on the White House.

After the inauguration of President Polk in March, the Tylers retired to their Virginia plantation, Sherwood Forest—Tyler's tongue-in-cheek reference to his outlaw status in politics. Julia dedicated herself to creating an elegant home for herself, her husband, and the seven children she would have over the next fourteen years. Still, she missed the excitement of Washington and the prestige of being First Lady. "I . . . have been almost spoiled by excitement and livelier scenes," Julia wrote wistfully to her mother. "What dinner parties of the usual kind in country or city would not appear dull to me after all those brilliant ones we gave at the White House."

The abrupt transition from the national limelight to the relative obscurity of country living failed to tame Julia's celebrated spirit, nor did it reduce her appetite for fine clothes. She continued to pay close attention to her wardrobe, and to shop by proxy for herself, her children, and her home via her family in New York. In order to keep intact this lifeline to Julia's family—and the latest styles—the Tylers tried to manage one trip a year to New York. Every trip necessitated a large outlay of funds, and Julia soon became famous for her shopping excursions in Richmond and New York. At one point, her oldest son, David Gardiner Tyler, complained, "A few more days of shopping would, I have no doubt, have made me a fit inmate of the Lunatic Asylum at Staunton."

Julia's undiminished passion for clothes was matched by a physical demeanor that seemed impervious to the effects of domesticity. While her figure grew fuller after numerous pregnancies, her resistance to aging nonetheless remained a source of admiration and wonder. Edmund Ruffin, the Virginia secessionist and agriculturist who would soon fire the first shot of the Civil War at Fort Sumter, wrote of Julia as she appeared when in her mid-thirties: "The mother of five living children, she still looks as blooming and fresh as a girl of twenty, and indeed I should not have guessed her to be older, if meeting her without knowing who she was . . ."

For all the apparent frivolity of her shopping sprees, and despite her departure from Washington, Julia continued to champion her husband's political causes, always referring to him as "the President" and to herself as "Mrs. Ex-President Tyler." She became an outspoken advocate for southern rights and in 1853 attracted national attention when she publicly responded to a letter penned by the duchess of Sutherland. On behalf of British women, the duchess had urged the women of the American South to bring an end to slavery. Julia harshly criticized the duchess, arguing that the English had no right to interfere in what she contended was an American domestic matter. The incident was immortalized in the lyrics to the song "Oh Susanna!":

Oh, Lady Sutherland,
To comfort you I'll try.
Mrs. Tyler gave you what was right,
But Duchess don't you cry.

In 1861, as the Union began to break apart and the country descended into war, Julia and John Tyler returned to Washington for the first time since their retirement. President Tyler had been invited to preside over the Peace Convention intended to stave off a full-scale war. While her seventy-one-year-old husband made efforts to preserve the Union, Julia set out to reconquer the capital. She was thrilled to see that she still drew crowds virtually everywhere she went. Exuberantly immodest as ever, Julia wrote her mother, "You ought to hear the compliments that are heaped upon me. I haven't changed a bit except to improve." In contrast to Julia's social triumphs, the Peace Convention failed to stop the coming war. The following year, John Tyler died of a stroke, and Julia continued to mourn her husband and defend his career for the rest of her life. She endured the hardships of the Civil War at her mother's home in Staten Island, and despite her northern roots remained a strong supporter of the Confederacy, sending supplies to her friends in Virginia.

Financially crippled by the war, Julia was determined to obtain a presidential widow's pension, seeking compensation equal to that which Congress had awarded Mary Todd Lincoln. Julia's sons, who had served in the Confederate army, were horrified to see their mother pander to the enemy, but Julia—passionate but always pragmatic—understood that hostilities had to be put aside if her family was going to survive and thrive once more. Seemingly undaunted by the strife of previous years, Julia continued to charm Washington society. She described one party in a letter to her oldest son: "I went, and the consequence was the handsomest

attentions . . . as the ladies crowded in at the reception and were introduced to me as 'Mrs. Ex-President Tyler.' I was enthusiastically received by those who had formerly met me and . . . I was taken by surprise . . . at the warmth of my old acquaintances—with the gulf of so many years between." In 1881, Congress approved an annual pension of five thousand dollars for all surviving presidential widows. This financial security eased Julia's worries about her future, and, at sixty-one, Julia Gardiner Tyler, in preparation for the summer social season in Newport, Rhode Island, did what came most naturally to her: she went shopping.

Julia's remaining years were spent in Richmond, Virginia, where she had leased a house, and where she remained a popular society figure and a darling of the press until her death on July 10, 1889. Julia Gardiner Tyler brought a singular style and youthful vigor to the office of President, a seat so often fraught with the dour business of state. She handled personal crises with great aplomb and left an indelible mark on her husband's administration. As official hostess, Julia Tyler instilled a degree of panache into White House social activities that had not been seen in Washington since the heyday of Dolley Madison. And yet she earned perhaps her greatest accolades by doing precisely the opposite of what was expected—assuming the dual role of iconoclast and celebrity in an era when conformity and propriety dominated.

Julia Gardiner Tyler, conscious of her public image,
sat for this daguerreotype. She was the first
President's wife to be captured by the camera.

Harriet Lane Johnston

Perhaps the greatest testament to the remarkable personality of Harriet Lane Johnston is that, as the United States descended into the chaos of the Civil War, she managed to distract a weary nation with the deep décolletage of her Paris gowns. In its outward aspect, the story of Harriet Lane is very much about style and fashion—about bringing refined, sensual European sensibilities to an American public still struggling with the prim idiosyncrasies of the Victorian era. At the heart of this singular woman, however, was a dignity and perseverance that nowadays is seldom associated with the glamorous, ephemeral persona of a fashion icon. As an attractive young woman with a taste for haute couture, Harriet Lane found getting attention easy. But she went a step further: she fundamentally changed the way women dressed in the middle of the nineteenth century, and in the process changed the minds and won the hearts of many.

At the age of twenty-six, Harriet Lane was handed one of the most difficult jobs in the country: to entertain Washington society on the eve of the Civil War. While her uncle, President James Buchanan, struggled with threats of secession and mounting political turmoil, Harriet, as the President's official hostess, succeeded in reestablishing the White House as a sanctuary in the nation's capital. Harriet Lane brought to the executive mansion the sophistication of the British aristocracy (and an elaborate Parisian wardrobe) that was strongly influenced by her days as a diplomatic consort in the court of England's Queen Victoria. Thanks in part to her experience in Europe, she became an ambassador of bold new styles that instantly found legions of imitators among the women who devoured the detailed press accounts of

Harriet Lane's gracious manner and European wardrobe captivated fashionable American women at a pivotal time, when the media began to target a female audience. This photograph captures her uncommon elegance.

her wardrobe. Inevitably, the new look Harriet embraced—a revealing off-the-shoulder neckline with deep décolletage—caused much hand-wringing among arbiters of taste, yet the sheer force of her personal demeanor easily propelled her above the clamor, ensuring that the styles of the First Lady would soon become those of the nation.

She was born on May 9, 1830, the youngest child of Jane Buchanan and Elliott T. Lane, in Mercersberg, Pennsylvania. Her family was wealthy, having made their fortune in the mercantile trade, selling supplies to settlers heading to Ohio. After both parents died, the young Harriet asked to live with her bachelor uncle, James Buchanan. When he became Harriet's legal guardian, Buchanan was a U.S. senator representing Pennsylvania.

Buchanan was very fond of Harriet and raised her as if she were his own daughter. But his life in politics called him away from home a great deal, and Harriet, left in the care of his housekeeper, was an independent child. Well-educated at private boarding schools, Harriet was a mischievous tomboy who balked at the discipline her teachers attempted to instill in her. She wrote letters to her uncle complaining about "the strict rules, early hours, brown sugar in the tea and restrictions in dress."

At sixteen, she was sent to Georgetown Visitation Convent, a prestigious finishing school in Washington, and on weekends she would visit her uncle, who by that time had become secretary of state to President James K. Polk. James Buchanan prepared his niece to be wise about politics, and she became an astute observer. On her visits home, he would have her sit in while he and his friends engaged in debate, grooming her for the world in which he lived. Charming and vivacious, she thoroughly relished company. It was during her years at finishing school that Harriet was befriended by Dolley Madison, who was by that time a venerated fixture on the Washington social circuit. It is a measure of Harriet's budding social acumen that she recognized the value of Dolley's favor, and she often called on Mrs. Madison during school holidays.

Harriet at eighteen was an attractive and intelligent young woman who displayed a sincere, even fervent desire to become a part of her uncle's world. In 1848, she graduated from Georgetown with high honors. A year later, she and Buchanan moved into Wheatland, a country estate outside of Lancaster, Pennsylvania. For the first time, the skills and graces that Harriet had cultivated were put to full use, and she proved an excellent hostess to the numerous dignitaries and officials who visited her uncle. She also became Buchanan's closest confidante, privy to his political aspirations and most guarded opinions. Evidently, Harriet could counterbalance her vivacious and outgoing manner with calm discretion when the occasion demanded.

Her unusual degree of maturity was sufficient to convince Buchanan to allow a well-chaperoned Harriet to attend the 1850 winter social season in Washington. Her uncle remained concerned about the prospect of his young and impressionable niece plunging into the intrigues of Washington society. "Keep your eyes about you in the gay scenes through which you are destined to pass and take care to do nothing and say nothing of which you may have cause to repent," he wrote. "Above all, be on your guard against flattery. Should you receive it, let it pass into one ear gracefully, and out at the other. Many a clever girl has been spoiled for the useful purposes of life . . . by a winter's gaiety in Washington."

GODEY'S UNRIVALLED COLORED FASHIONS.
1855

When Buchanan was named ambassador to Great Britain in 1853, Harriet pleaded to go with him, but he insisted she remain at Wheatland until he summoned her. As always, he mixed a stuffy dose of fatherly concern with a measure of genuine sympathy for the needs of his young niece; he relented the following year, stipulating that she pay her own expenses with the money from her inheritance.

She arrived in London that spring. Twenty-four-year-old Harriet was a rare beauty, possessed of a thick mass of golden hair, deep blue eyes, and a glowing complexion. Admired for her regal posture and effortless grace, Harriet was equally acclaimed for her lively personality and intelligence. In short, she was the belle of London's diplomatic world. She quickly became a favorite of Queen Victoria and the royal family, and was awarded the privileged rank of Ambassador's Consort—an unusual honor for the female relative of a diplomat. In this elevated capacity, Harriet was invited to attend public functions of the court, as well as intimate dinners with Queen Victoria and Prince Albert, who called her "Dear Miss Lane."

While in London, she frequently wrote letters to her sister Mary, who had married and moved to San Francisco. These letters shed light on her role as official hostess at the American embassy and her life at Queen Victoria's court. As a member of the American ambassador's household whose duties brought her into regular contact with royalty, Harriet had to obtain a wardrobe that conformed to a strict dress code before she could be presented to the queen. The situation apparently merited a shopping spree in Paris, which was then the undisputed fashion center of Europe, in no small part thanks to the stylish Empress Eugénie, wife of Napoleon III, and her court. While in the French capital, Harriet indulged in the latest fashions. During the 1850s, the long heavy lines that had defined the

fashions of Europe and America during the previous decade were replaced by a lighter silhouette featuring bell-shaped skirts supported by numerous layers of starched and ruffled petticoats; tightly fitted bodices, which showed off the corseted waistlines of the era; and pagoda sleeves, cut full from elbow to wrist, so named for the Chinese structure they resembled. One of the most popular styles for women's dresses during Harriet's time in London featured a flounced skirt, which often had fringed trim along the edge of the flounces, sleeves, and bodice. After splurging on her wardrobe in France, an exuberant Harriet wrote her sister Mary of the fashions she had seen: "Everything is worn in Paris standing out. Skirts cannot be too full and stiff; sleeves are still open, and basque [bodices], either open in front or closed; flounces are very much worn. I had some dresses made in Paris that I wish you could see." She was now squarely at the center of the grand aristocratic social firmament of Europe.

One of the many challenges of regularly attending the English court was to be ready for unplanned events—such as celebrating the birth or mourning the death of a royal relation—and the tiresome shifts in dress and protocol any given event might entail. In an era of custom-made clothes, having the proper dress readied on short notice necessitated a small team of seamstresses working late into the night. To her sister Mary, Harriet recounted the emergency of a dinner invitation from the queen: "As the court [was] in mourning, and I had no black dress, one day's notice kept me very busy. I ought to have black dresses, for the court is often in mourning, and you know I belong to it; but the season being quiet, I did not expect to go to any court parties."

Among the many gowns Harriet commissioned, the most elaborate were those designed for attending the queen's salons. For these occasions, court protocol required women to wear an evening gown, a headdress of

"Unless required to present Americans," Harriet wrote to her sister Mary, "I shall not go more than twice this year [to the salon]. It is expensive—one cannot wear the same dress twice." Harriet may initially have been enthralled by the royal splendor of Buckingham Palace, as shown at left, but by no means was she entirely under its spell.

white ostrich feathers with a lace veil, and a train suspended from either the shoulders or the waist. Since the trains could be as long as eleven feet, women assiduously practiced maneuvering in them to avoid an embarrassing slip when walking backward away from Her Majesty after curtseying. Harriet described to her sister the gown she wore to a royal salon in 1855: "I wore a pink silk petticoat, over-skirts of pink tulle, puffed and trimmed with wreaths of apple blossoms; a train of pink silk, trimmed with blonde [lace] and apple blossoms . . . [and a] headdress of apple blossoms, lace lappets, and feathers." That afternoon she must have made a remarkable impression on the crowd—while returning home from the salon, her taciturn uncle was said to have managed the following accolade: "Well, a person would have supposed you were a great beauty, to have heard the way you were talked of today."

While in England, she was courted by many men, both young and old. Even the queen played matchmaker, encouraging her to marry a member of the court so she could remain in London. From an early age, however, Harriet had been advised by Buchanan to select a husband with caution. "It is my desire," he told her, "that you shall exercise your own judgment in the choice of a husband. View steadily all the consequences, ask the guidance of Heaven, and make up your own mind." While she flirted with a number of men in London, she did not seriously consider any of their proposals. Once again, she displayed an almost glib levelheadedness in the face of a dazzling array of temptations and opportunities.

Following Buchanan's nomination as the Democratic Party candidate for President in April of 1856, Harriet put her skills to work once again, entertaining politicians and supporters at her uncle's home. In March of 1857, after his victory, Harriet accompanied her uncle to Washington to serve as his official hostess in the White House. After watching Buchanan take the oath of office and observing a large parade in the new President's honor, she accompanied him to the inaugural ball, which was held in a building that had been constructed exclusively for the event at a

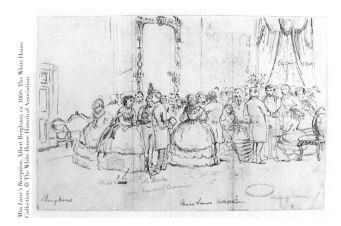

Before photojournalism, artists sketched public events for newspapers and magazines. This pencil drawing from 1860, "Miss Lane's Reception at the White House," provided viewers with an intimate look into Harriet's world.

cost of fifteen thousand dollars. The six thousand guests were entertained by a forty-piece orchestra and were served a lavish supper of oysters, mutton, ham, jellies, ice cream, and slices from a four-foot-high cake. Harriet was resplendent in a white evening gown festooned with flowers and accented by a pearl necklace. The following day, newspapers hailed her as "Our Democratic Queen."

During Buchanan's administration, there was a surge in the number of newspapers in the country, along with a corresponding surge in the number of journalists reporting on events in Washington. Female readership was on the rise, and newspapers catered to this expanding constituency by featuring news on Harriet Lane and social activities at the White House. For the first time, newspapers referred to the President's hostess as "the First Lady." *Frank Leslie's Illustrated Newspaper* wrote in March of 1860, under a full-page illustration of Harriet, "The subject of our illustration, from the semi-official position

The elegant, mid-nineteenth-century sway of women's skirts was a product of the cage crinoline, a steel wire frame that supported the yards of fabric used in fashionable attire.

which she has so long sustained with so much honor to herself and credit to her country may be justly termed the First Lady in the land." This unofficial title swiftly worked its way into the nation's vocabulary.

Having come to respect the abilities she displayed while stationed in London, Buchanan put Harriet in charge of all the social duties and obligations of the office of President. He also turned over to her the responsibility of refurbishing the White House—an expense covered by a recently approved Congressional appropriation. She was the youngest woman to serve as White House hostess since twenty-five-year-old Betty Taylor Bliss had performed these duties from 1848 to 1850 for her invalid mother, Margaret, the wife of President Zachary Taylor. Harriet's youthful enthusiasm quickly captured the public imagination. With more illustrated press accounts than ever at their disposal, women began to copy Harriet's style of dress.

The year 1856 had witnessed a major innovation in women's fashions—the development of the cage crinoline. The crinoline—or hoop, as it was also known—was made of concentric steel rings, increasing in diameter from waist to hem and attached to one another by woven cotton tapes; the crinoline provided greater ease of movement for women by allowing them to discard the cumbersome layers of petticoats they had been wearing to support their voluminous skirts. The drawback was that moving about in the new invention required some practice. Also, the crinoline could take on a life of its own if caught by a gust of wind. So women began wearing trouser-style undergarments known as pantaloons, which provided a layer of modesty should the crinoline suddenly reveal more of the wearer than was socially desirable. The same year also saw the development of chemical dyes, which completely changed the palette of fashion. Women embraced the new, stunningly vibrant colors, which replaced the muted shades derived from natural sources that had been used for centuries. It is more than probable that Harriet Lane adopted both of these innovations during her tenure in the White House. Her particular contribution to American fashion during this period, however, was the popularization of low-necked gowns and bertha collars. The bertha collar was a deep flounce of lace that softly edged the neckline of an evening bodice and was a perfect complement to the voluminous skirts created by a cage crinoline. The collar provided a sense of balance for the silhouette, and as Harriet was admired for her beautiful neck and shoulders, this style suited her figure perfectly.

With secessionist tensions simmering and near-brawls erupting in Congress over the question of slavery, Harriet's duties as First Lady required almost superhuman diplomatic skill. Buchanan determined the guest lists for dinners and receptions and left it to his niece to find seating plans that would neither violate protocol nor place enemies too close to one another. Clever enough to avoid entanglement in partisan skirmishes, Harriet floated delicately just above the political fray. And despite the foreboding atmosphere in Washington, she thoroughly enjoyed her role as First Lady. Her White House was the nerve center of Washington society, as she kept its guests amused and congenial, even amid political chaos.

Harriet's first reception in the White House was a great success, and so was she. In a front-page story, *The New York Times* noted, "In appearance and tone she has the most marked characteristics of the well-bred Englishwoman, being a bright blonde, and exhibiting the traces of that gushing health and its attending vivacity which form almost a part of English education. This training in a responsible position abroad, and the habit of society to which she has been accustomed at Wheatland . . . have put her quite at home in the White

An 1858 Harper's Weekly *featured the background image on this page, which was most likely based on the daguerreotype above. At about that time, Harriet Lane became the first presidential hostess to be referred to in print as "First Lady."*

House. The impression to-day [sic] was altogether successful, and Miss Lane is evidently destined to acquire a social popularity which will vie with that which Mrs. Bliss left as an example seven years ago."

In England, Harriet had met philanthropists and art patrons, and this exposure informed her outspoken support of social and cultural causes in America. Wealthy friends and acquaintances soon followed her example. She became an important patron of the arts herself, going so far as to invite artists to White House dinners, a practice previously unheard of, and to lobby Congress for the establishment of a national gallery. She also took a serious interest in the welfare of Native Americans, using her power as de facto presidential advisor to influence legislation. Hailed as "Great Mother of the Indians," Harriet worked to improve conditions in tribal communities and personally responded to their appeals for assistance. Buchanan took great pride in his niece's efforts.

As political tensions in the country mounted, President Buchanan lost the support of his party. He became increasingly aloof and irritable, and by 1859 the burdens of the office created friction between Harriet and her uncle. They fought over his refusal to allow dancing in the White House and over his constant opening and reading of her private correspondence. That summer she left the White House for a three-month vacation. The President tersely told friends, "I do not care how long she stays [away], I can do very well without her."

As political quarreling intensified, the numerous attacks leveled by Buchanan's opponents in the press soon targeted the First Lady as well. She was roundly criticized in the newspapers for taking friends on a cruise up the Hudson River in the *Harriet Lane*, a cutter belonging to the government that was named in her honor by the secretary of the treasury. This youthful indiscretion was characterized by the press as an abuse of presidential privilege and a waste of the taxpayers' money. Buchanan, unable to remain cross for long at his adored niece, offered words of compassion. "I am sorry to find that your excursion to West Point on the *Harriet Lane* has been made the subject of newspaper criticism on yourself. This is most ungallant and ungentlemanly."

In the fall of 1860, the nation enjoyed a welcome—if fleeting—respite from its troubles when the Prince of Wales paid an informal visit to Washington. Queen Victoria had given permission for her oldest son to visit America on his return from a tour of Canada, and the pomp of royalty offered distraction to a public weary of bad news. Harriet served as the prince's official escort, and while her uncle would not permit any dancing in the White House, she danced with the future king of England at a reception at the British minister's home.

In 1860, Abraham Lincoln was elected the nation's sixteenth President, and James Buchanan began preparing for his retirement from public office. Harriet hosted the last levee of the administration on February 12, 1861, and it was considered by all to be the most brilliant social occasion of the previous four years.

Harriet returned to Wheatland with her uncle that same year. In 1865, she announced that she would marry Henry Elliott Johnston, a lawyer from Baltimore whom she had met in Bedford Springs, Pennsylvania, when she was nineteen. They were married at Wheatland on January 11, 1866, by Buchanan's brother, Reverend Edward Buchanan, in front of a small group of family and friends. She wore a gown of white silk moiré, with her trademark neckline edged in lace and satin, and a pointed scalloped hem with a chapel train.

After a honeymoon in Cuba, Harriet and Henry Johnston settled in Baltimore. In November, their first child was born, and they named him after the ex-President. Buchanan was thrilled to become a great-uncle; his letters fondly illustrate the keen interest he took in his infant namesake. In 1868, James Buchanan died at Wheatland, leaving the estate to Harriet. A year later, she gave birth to her second child, Henry Elliott Johnston, Jr. Both her sons were of a delicate constitution, and in 1881 the older boy died of rheumatic fever. Harriet and her husband took their surviving son to the south of France in hopes that the warm climate would improve his health, but he, too, died, in 1882. Two years later, Henry died in New York, while receiving medical treatment for a lingering illness. Alone, Harriet sold both her Baltimore home and Wheatland and settled in Washington.

Only fifty-four years old, Harriet Lane Johnston was the sole surviving member of her family. She had seen her parents, siblings, uncle, sons, and husband succumb to disease. Thereafter, she lived in near seclusion, periodically making extended journeys to Europe, where she took pleasure in pursuing her passion for collecting fine art. She found relief from her enormous tragedies by throwing herself into cherished social causes. She became a champion of children's issues, laying the groundwork for a hospital that would specialize in the treatment of chronically ill children. With her sponsorship of Saint Alban's Choir School at the National Cathedral in Washington, she provided funds for the building of classrooms and dormitories, and for scholarships in memory of her sons. She also befriended her successors in the White House, attending receptions as a special guest and dispensing advice in the grand tradition of Dolley Madison.

At her death in 1903, Harriet bequeathed her art collection to the government with the stipulation that a national gallery of art be founded for the preservation and collection of works of fine art. The seed she planted in 1903 ultimately grew to be one of the world's great museums. She left the bulk of her fortune to Johns Hopkins University for the creation, in memory of her sons, of a hospital dedicated to universal medical care for children, regardless of race, religion, or financial situation. Known for years as the Harriet Lane Home for Invalid Children, the hospital is now part of the world-renowned Johns Hopkins Children's Center.

It is remarkable that such lasting philanthropic achievements could be matched by an equally profound impact in the less tangible realm of personal style. Virginia Clay, the wife of a southern senator during Buchanan's administration, reminisced on Harriet's four years as First Lady: "The charms of young womanhood still lingered about her, but to these was added an aplomb rare in a woman of fifty, so that, during her residence in it, White House functions rose to their highest degree of elegance; to a standard, indeed, that has not since been approached." Harriet Lane Johnston inspired women throughout mid-nineteenth-century America with the fashions she popularized and the causes she championed. Her lively personality, natural grace, and elegant fashions appealed to women, and they in turn looked to her as the embodiment of enlightened Victorian womanhood: adoring niece, charming national hostess, and loving wife and mother. In the end, what placed Harriet Lane

In 1878, artist John Henry Brown captured the enduring elegance of the former First Lady. Though the bertha collar had passed out of favor, Harriet Lane remained loyal to its flattering qualities.

Johnston in the pantheon of great American women was her singular ability to balance a lifelong passion for all things fine and elegant with a heartfelt love for all things human.

Frances Folsom Cleveland Preston

Frances Folsom Cleveland, whose life
many perceived to be a fairy tale in the
making, was perhaps the first American woman
to be truly engulfed by the role of "celebrity" in the contemporary sense of the word. Unlike her predecessor
Julia Tyler, who openly courted publicity, Frances was
the reluctant recipient of the excessive attentions of both
the media, which began to wield enormous power in the
late nineteenth century, and the general public.

Frances Folsom was a month shy of her twenty-
second birthday when she married President Grover
Cleveland in the Blue Room of the White House in 1886.
In just one day, she was transformed from a relatively
anonymous college graduate into the nation's youngest
First Lady. She came of age when the country had just
begun to enjoy the fruits of the postwar Reconstruction,
and when the national press was bolder, less scrupulous,
and more accessible to the average citizen than ever
before. From the moment she relocated to the executive
mansion, her every move—from her choice of hats to
the slightest fluctuation in hairstyle—was reported by
the press and subsequently copied by women around
the country.

The events of Frances Cleveland's life both echoed
society's longing for the grandeur of Dolley Madison's
days and foreshadowed the national obsession that
attended the lives of Jacqueline Kennedy Onassis and
Diana, Princess of Wales. Like both Diana and Jackie,
Frances Cleveland made the grim discovery that
celebrity, for better or worse, is always built on appearances. Even her husband could not afford to ignore the
power of the First Lady's image, and reluctantly agreed
to include her face on his 1888 campaign button. And

*Frances Folsom Cleveland was only twenty-two years
old when she married President Grover Cleveland in
1886 and assumed the mantle of First Lady.*

when Frances Cleveland's social achievements elevated her above the realm of fashion, as they often did, they were inevitably lost in clamorous accounts of her wardrobe and social agenda. Before long, her face was co-opted by countless entrepreneurs, who traded upon her name and image to sell everything from perfume to candy. Frances Folsom Cleveland had crossed over, via the power of image and the fairy-tale trappings of fashion, from the world of a mere celebrity to the realm of a national icon.

Frances Folsom could not remember a time when she did not know Grover Cleveland. Her father, Oscar, came from a large, wealthy family that lived outside Buffalo, New York, where he and Cleveland were partners in a law firm. On July 21, 1864, when Oscar's wife, Emma, gave birth to their first and only child, Frances Clara, Cleveland was one of the first to visit the infant. "Uncle Cleve" even bought a baby carriage for "Frank," as the little girl was soon called.

In July of 1874, Frank's world changed forever: her father was killed when the horse-drawn carriage he was driving overturned at high speed. As the family mourned, Grover Cleveland was appointed executor of his best friend's estate. Because of his fondness for Emma and Frank, he remained part of their personal lives as well, providing whatever assistance they required, though Oscar had left his widow and ten-year-old daughter a handsome inheritance.

In 1882, Frank entered Wells College, where she majored in French and German, thriving in the collegiate atmosphere. At Wells, the fondness Frances Folsom and Grover Cleveland felt for each other developed into something more personal. Frank had become a bright, stunning young woman, and Cleveland had fallen under her spell. Showing great tact, Cleveland requested permission from Emma Folsom to correspond with Frank while she was away at college. Then governor of New York, Grover Cleveland sent letters every week, accompanied by flowers from the greenhouses at the governor's mansion.

Cleveland ran for President in 1884 on the Democratic ticket. In the first salvo of what became a long battle between Cleveland and the press, radical elements of the Republican Party published reports during the campaign that the governor had an illegitimate son. Cleveland met the smear with a composed, honest response: he acknowledged that he had helped support the child of a woman he once knew, one Maria Halprin, but that he did not know if the child was his. Throughout this scandal, the Folsom women stood by Cleveland, impressed with his honesty. He weathered the storm and that November was elected the nation's twenty-second President. The scandal, however, prefigured the battles his administration would be forced to wage against an emboldened, often intrusive, national press.

Grover Cleveland was the first bachelor to occupy the White House since James Buchanan, and the press was eager to marry him off. He had all the outward appearances of a confirmed bachelor: most tellingly, he preferred fishing with his male friends to socializing in the company of women. His sister once asked him if he had ever thought of getting married, and he responded, "A good many times; and the more I think of it the more I think I'll not do it." When asked the same question a few years later, however, Cleveland had apparently softened his position: "I'm only waiting for my wife to grow up," he said slyly.

Frances and Emma Folsom were not able to attend Grover Cleveland's inauguration because it conflicted with final exams at school; but as soon as spring break arrived, the Folsoms were off to Washington to visit the family friend who by then held the highest office in the land. Cleveland was a noted workaholic, but during Emma and Frank's two-week visit he took time from his schedule to go driving with Frank and take evening walks with her around the White House's formal rooms. What had begun as familial affection and later evolved into a delicate campaign of long-distance letter-writing appeared to be taking shape as courtship in earnest—on the grounds of the executive mansion, no less.

A few months after her White House visit, Cleveland sent a letter of proposal to Frank. She enthusiastically accepted and wanted to be married right away, but was eventually persuaded by her mother, and the President himself, that she should do some traveling and think it over. In September, when Frank and her mother stayed at the White House before setting sail for Europe, the visit provoked rumors that the chief executive was about to marry. Proving that gossip was easier to come by than hard facts, newspapers mistakenly reported that Cleveland was soon to wed Mrs. Folsom. Cleveland, whose long-standing friendship with Emma allowed occasional good-natured ribbing, responded to the flood of erroneous newspaper reports with characteristic panache: "I don't see why the papers keep marrying me to old ladies." Again, the curiosity of the press and the public was piqued.

While in Europe, the Folsoms traveled to Paris to purchase Frank's wedding gown and the other elements of her trousseau. In the late nineteenth century, Paris remained the mecca of world fashion, as a result of the tremendously popular innovations of one man: the Paris-based, English-born couturier and father of haute couture, Charles Frederick Worth. His salon was patronized by the most fashionable, aristocratic women in Europe, including Empress Eugénie, and by the enormously wealthy Americans who dominated post–Civil War high society. During her sojourn in Paris, Frank paid a visit to the House of Worth and ordered a suitably elegant dress for her upcoming nuptials.

As Frank and her mother prepared to return to New York in May of 1886, the press, still convinced that marriage was afoot, stayed on their trail. They escaped being plagued by journalists during their return journey only by insisting upon an anonymous booking on the ship's manifest. To save his fiancée from a mob of reporters at the dock in New York, Cleveland arranged for Frank and her mother to be met in New York harbor by a government boat, which took them to a separate port, where

Frances Cleveland was often photographed wearing this small pin in the shape of her favorite flower, the pansy.

they could enter the country undetected. With the exception of heads of state fearful of assassination, few public figures had ever been forced to go to such lengths to shield themselves from public view.

While Frank was abroad, Cleveland had been planning their wedding. "I want my marriage to be a quiet one and am determined that the American Sovereigns [the press] shall not interfere with a thing so purely personal to me," he told his sister Mary. It was decided that the marriage would take place at the home of Frank's grandfather, away from the Washington press corps, but news arrived that he had died just as Frank and Emma were returning from Europe. While this unexpected misfortune caused a sudden hitch in the wedding plans, it helped to ensure that the nuptials remained private. Mourning customs of the era dictated that out of respect for the deceased, weddings held shortly after the death of a family member should be small. The bridal party was permitted to put aside their mourning clothes for the ceremony, but had to resume wearing black immediately afterward. As for the venue, however, Cleveland wished most of all to provide his young bride with a beautiful wedding. So he decided that the ceremony would be held in the White House—press be damned.

Once the White House had announced the President's forthcoming marriage to Frank, the press covered every detail of the approaching nuptials. Frank's trousseau was the subject of a front-page story in *The New York Times*, which provided minute details on the cut, color, and embellishments of her Parisian wardrobe. At seven o'clock on the evening of June 2, 1886, Frances Folsom, escorted by the groom, entered the Blue Room of the White House as Mendelssohn's "Wedding March," played by John Philip Sousa's Marine Band, announced their approach to the altar. In a ten-minute ceremony attended by only twenty-nine people—including friends, family, and Cabinet members—they were married. The moment the ceremony was completed, a twenty-one-gun salute rang out from the Navy Yard, and the peal of church bells was heard throughout the capital.

Crowds and reporters filled the White House lawn as they tried to get a look at the bride through the mansion's windows. Before the wedding, *The Washington Post*, perhaps anticipating criticism of the press frenzy, had run an editorial: "Everybody is gossiping about the White House wedding. Men and women are interested in an affair which has never before been witnessed and the curiosity manifested is neither vulgar nor impertinent: it is merely the penalty which those occupying high stations always have to pay." Regardless of whether the public agreed with the *Post*'s assessment, Americans relished the grandeur of this event down to its smallest details, and were thrilled to witness the trappings of a "royal" wedding on their own shores.

The bride's gown was fashioned of heavy-ribbed ivory silk, with the then-ubiquitous bustled skirt, a fifteen-foot train, and a high-necked tailored bodice with form-fitting, three-quarter-length sleeves. The bodice, skirt, and sleeves were trimmed with orange blossoms, the most popular bridal flower of the nineteenth century. On her head Frank wore a veil of silk tulle, but she carried no bouquet and wore no jewelry. After a reception and dinner for their guests, Cleveland and his new bride were spirited from the White House to begin their honeymoon in Deer Park, Maryland. The intrepid press soon caught up with them and camped out around the honeymoon cottage, using binoculars and telescopes to spy on the newlyweds.

Once back at the White House, Cleveland sent off an angry missive to *The New York Evening Post*, blasting the press for their invasive tactics: "They have used the enormous powers of the modern newspaper," he wrote, "to perpetuate and disseminate a colossal impertinence, and have done it, not as professional gossips and tattlers, but as the guides and instruments of the public in conduct and morals. And they have done it, not to a private citizen, but to the President of the United States, thereby lifting their offense into the gaze of the whole world, and doing their utmost to make American journalism contemptible in the estimation of people of good breeding everywhere." From good-natured, if prickly, tolerance of the press, the President's tone had shifted to outright indignation.

The newly married Clevelands held two receptions after they returned from their honeymoon—one for the

A *small, private affair in the Blue Room of the White House, the wedding of President Grover Cleveland and Frances Folsom created a media frenzy that continued long after the honeymoon was over. The bridal gown of ivory silk (right) had been purchased from the noted French couturier Charles Frederick Worth.*

MAGASIN DES DEMOISELLES

47, RUE LAFFITTE, PARIS

25 Décembre

Parfumerie Oriza de L.LEGRAND f.ᵉ des Cours de Russie et d'Italie, r. S.ᵗ Honoré, 207.

VELOUTINE FAY r DE LA PAIX 9.

diplomatic corps and the other for the public. Frank wore her wedding gown on both occasions, but without her veil and with the addition of a diamond necklace her husband had given her as a wedding gift. In the course of two evenings she shook the hands of more than ten thousand people. Everyone who met the young bride was impressed. At twenty-two, she was tall, slim, and graceful, with large blue eyes, a creamy complexion, and thick, wavy brown hair.

Almost overnight, Frances Cleveland had been transformed from a schoolgirl ingenue into the nation's First Lady. She was the most celebrated—and the most copied—woman in the country. Her every move was documented in the newspapers. Men adored her and women emulated her. Without hesitation, she was dubbed the most popular First Lady since Dolley Madison. Thousands of photographs of her were sold and displayed in homes throughout the country, and women began to wear their hair "à la Cleveland," copying the bun Frank wore in an unusually low position at the nape of her neck. Every public appearance was chronicled in the press, including elaborate descriptions of her dresses. These news reports detailed richly trimmed day dresses, brightly colored in the popular palette of the era: violet velvet, pale-blue mohair, moss-green plush, and blue silk with a rosebud brocade. These dresses were made in the prevailing style: plain, tailored bodices and elaborately constructed full skirts with shelf-like bustles supporting the skirt in the back. Her evening gowns were predominantly white or ivory, and were adorned with gold embroidery, feathers, and other fine decorations. While the style of the day was a fairly covered-up look, in the evenings women wore sleeveless bodices that were little more than a cover for their corsets, with necklines that plunged in both front and back.

Recognizing the First Lady's tremendous influence on fashion, the National Women's Temperance Convention saw an opportunity to further its pious mission: the convention asked the First Lady to set an example for young women throughout the country by abstaining from the revealing décolletage that was rapidly becoming de rigueur for women's evening wear. The First Lady chose to politely ignore the convention's request, as she ignored the many compromising public remarks issued by the press, and continued to dress as she pleased.

In addition to intense media scrutiny, Frank soon faced a relatively new problem. In a country where commerce was bustling once again after years of wartime stagnation, disreputable advertisers began to exploit the First Lady's wholesome image to sell their products. Her face appeared on ads for products ranging from perfume and candy to liver pills. One particularly offensive company advertised that the First Lady's beautiful complexion was the result of eating arsenic, eliciting the following response from the President's secretary: "This is false from beginning to end. It is only a sample of many outrageous statements. Such things are exceedingly

The constricting corsets and elaborate skirts of the 1880s, depicted in the magazine illustration on the opposite page, made even simple movements complicated—although they apparently did not prevent women from enjoying a good game of billiards, as depicted in the engraving at left. Frances Cleveland's adoption of these revealing bodices caused concern among conservative women's groups.

Frances Cleveland's enormous popularity led to the exploitation of her image in advertisements for products ranging from mercerized thread to sulphur bitters. Note that two of these made free use of her official photograph (page 74). Frances was also featured as the Queen of Hearts on the cover of Judge *magazine in 1887.*

distasteful to Mrs. Cleveland. It is unnecessary to say that she has nothing to do with advertisements of any kind. She feels the responsibilities of her position as the wife of the President, and she has a right to expect the courtesy which is due it." To avoid entanglement in costly and embarrassing lawsuits, the First Lady simply kept her head up and tried her best to ignore the effusion of bad taste swirling around her.

In spite of these distractions, Grover Cleveland's marriage to Frank invigorated his presidency. In the fall of 1887, they toured the West and the South, meeting huge crowds at every stop. Frank shook so many hands each day that she had to have her hand iced and her arm massaged every evening. Occasionally, Frank's sudden appearance at a public event would cause the crowd to surge. When she appeared on a reviewing stand in Saint Louis, hundreds of people stormed forward, climbing stairs and walls to get a better look at her.

Energizing at first, the constant attention soon became suffocating. President Cleveland bought a house near Georgetown, called Oak View, which served as a retreat for the first couple. The Clevelands began to live there full time; the President commuted to the White House every day, while Frank returned to the executive residence only during the social season.

As the presidential election of 1888 drew near, Republican agitators, poised to commence the mudslinging that characterized the previous election, realized that if they attacked Frank there might be a huge public backlash. "[Frank's] popularity makes her the most potent factor in the administration which the Republicans have to face and fight against," a commentator noted. Although the First Lady might have been off-limits, the President himself was not. Opponents began to circulate wild rumors that Cleveland beat his wife and mother-in-law, and had on one occasion kicked Frank out of the White House in the middle of the night. To the contrary, all evidence suggests that the Clevelands were deeply in love, and they were shocked and horrified by the allegations. This time Frank refused to sit quietly; she wrote an open letter to the newspapers, refuting the rumors and defending her husband: "I can wish the women of our country no better blessing than that their homes and lives may be as happy, and that their husbands may be as kind and attentive, as considerate and affectionate, as mine."

The Clevelands may have preserved their dignity, but Grover Cleveland was unable to capture the vote. After conceding the race of 1888, the President and his wife made plans to retire to New York, where they hoped to become private citizens and avoid the limelight. Even so, as they left the White House on the day of Benjamin Harrison's inauguration, Frank is reported to have turned to one of the servants and said, "Now, Jerry, I want you to take good care of all the furniture and ornaments in the house, for I want to find everything just as it is now when we come back again." During their time in New York, Frank gave birth to their first child, Ruth, whose arrival into the world caused a media circus equal to that of her parents' wedding. One by-product of the media clamor remains with us today: the candy bar that was named in the little girl's honor, the Baby Ruth—a whimsical footnote to the Cleveland era.

In 1892, capitalizing on his residual popularity, Cleveland threw his hat in the ring once again and was elected to another term as President. Although he had discouraged campaign strategists from exploiting his wife's popularity, Frank's picture was included on posters, buttons, and other campaign materials as a complement to the pictures of her husband and his running mate. Female supporters of the Democratic Party even started Frances Cleveland Influence Clubs, much to the President's chagrin.

The woman who reassumed her duties as First Lady in March of 1893 was no longer the young college girl of four years earlier. Frank had matured and her self-confidence had developed significantly. Her clothes during this period were boldly patterned and richly colorful—typical of the era, but requiring a strong personality to carry off. Her gown for the inaugural ball was described in detail by *The New York Times*: "heavy white satin, [with an] empire front, and tight-fitting back. It was richly trimmed with point lace and embroidered with crystal beads. The embroidery ran up in rows, about twelve inches from the bottom of the skirt, which was pointed in the back. The empire waist was outlined with the lace and the crystal embroidery. The sleeves were

large puffs made of satin, dotted with the beads, and had stiff satin bows at the shoulders. A heavy fall of the lace completed the corsage."

Armed with experience, Frank handled her myriad social duties with great skill and charm. During Cleveland's first administration, she had instituted Saturday afternoon receptions intended to offer working women the pleasure of visiting the White House. She immediately reinstated this practice. Returning to the White House meant more than simply resuming old routines, however. Frank added to her responsibilities as First Lady those of raising a family. In 1893, Frank gave birth to a second daughter, Esther, the first child of a President to be born in the White House. Two years later, Marion was born. The adoration the public had previously reserved for Frank was lavished freely upon her children as well. Americans were fascinated by the Cleveland girls; the names Ruth, Esther, and Marion surged in popularity. One day not long after returning to the White House, Frank looked out the window to see one-year-old Ruth and her nurse being set upon by visitors. Frank immediately ordered the gates to the White House grounds closed to give her children some measure

Practical as well as stylish, Frances Cleveland had three different bodices made to coordinate with this printed floral chine skirt, which she wore during her second term as First Lady.

of privacy. This only fueled the fire of speculation, as newspapers, always quick with their reckless interpretations of events at the White House, suggested that Ruth might be deaf or mute.

During both of her husband's administrations, Frank championed causes important to her. She strongly supported higher education for women, viewing a college education as a woman's best chance for equality. She was also a staunch proponent of the kindergarten movement, which advocated introducing young children to the fundamentals of learning through educational toys, and even started a kindergarten in the White House. During the financial panic of 1893, she became actively involved in the Needlework Guild of America, encouraging women to make or purchase clothing for destitute families. Her philanthropic undertakings ultimately were of great service, but her stylish clothes, predictably, tended to command more attention than her social work.

In 1896, the Clevelands prepared to leave the White House for the last time. At her final Saturday reception for working women, more than three thousand guests came by to say farewell to Frank. On the day of McKinley's inauguration, she assembled her White House staff for the last time, thanking them for their good work during their two terms together. As hard as she tried, she was unable to hold back tears as she left the White House.

Hoping to stay out of the spotlight, but craving the activity of a college town, the Clevelands selected Princeton, New Jersey, as the site of their retirement. Two sons were born during this period. In 1904, the family suffered a crushing loss when Ruth died of diphtheria. Four years later, in 1908, after twenty-two years of marriage and a lifetime with Frank, Grover Cleveland died. The deaths of her daughter and husband within a four-year span were devastating to Frank. Remaining in the family home in Princeton, she lived a relatively secluded life, raising her four surviving children, whose ages ranged from five to fifteen years old at the time of their father's death.

In 1913, Frank remarried, taking as her husband Thomas Jex Preston, a professor at Wells College who had come to teach at Princeton University. Throughout the remainder of her life she continued to be active in the causes she loved, participating in the National Security League Speaker's Bureau during World War I and becoming president of the Needlework Guild, overseeing the collection of knitted clothing for the soldiers in Europe. During the Great Depression, she again used her name to encourage women throughout the country to help supply warm clothes to the needy.

In 1947, shortly before her death at the age of eighty-three—one depression and two world wars after she first set foot in the White House—Frank found herself once again in presidential company, this time in the person of Harry S. Truman. During his visit to Princeton for the University's bicentennial celebration, the President told Frank a story. His mother, he said, had once traveled many miles from their farm in rural Missouri all the way to Kansas City just to get a glimpse of Frances Cleveland in person; in his mother's scrapbook there was a yellowed newspaper clipping describing Mrs. Cleveland's heralded visit so many years before. Truman told Frank, "I am grateful to have met you, since now I can tell my mother that the real person surpasses even the person whom she imagined." Frances Cleveland Preston lived long enough to regain a measure of the anonymity she had lost when she married President Grover Cleveland in the White House. Yet she remained a cherished figure in the minds of an entire generation of Americans, her image symbolizing the grandeur of their era.

The President's wife as she appeared on the cover of The New York Times Magazine, *March 14, 1897—an accomplished First Lady at the end of her husband's second term.*

Alice Roosevelt Longworth

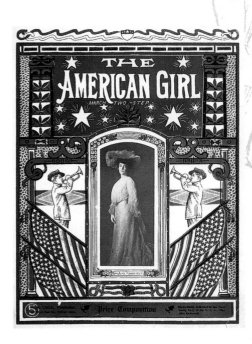

This photograph of Alice Roosevelt (left), taken at Sagamore Hill, the family home on Long Island, captures the striking beauty and powerful presence that made her a favorite with the American public. Alice's enormous popularity and resemblance to the Gibson Girl (shown in the background) inspired songwriters to celebrate her, in 1905, as "The American Girl."

With Queen Victoria's death in 1901, an era and a century came to a close. Americans ushered in a new society that would be increasingly manipulated by the power and influence of the media. Leading the nation into the twentieth century was the larger-than-life figure of Theodore Roosevelt, the charismatic statesman who became President when William McKinley was assassinated in 1901. Roosevelt had a restless energy and enthusiasm that captivated Americans and delighted the press. Here was a President who sought publicity as eagerly as he fought the trusts and monopolies that dominated American commerce. The only person in the country who consistently managed to steal headlines from him was his daughter Alice, who was seventeen years old when her father took office

Beautiful, independent, intelligent, and possessed of a complete disregard for social convention, Alice was a journalist's dream, always providing good copy, thanks to her unorthodox behavior in conservative Washington. She was photographed by the press everywhere she went, and every detail of her life was front-page news. Americans developed a cult-like fascination with the President's rebellious teenage daughter, who was seen as the epitome of the Gibson Girl—the Edwardian pinup created by graphic artist Charles Dana Gibson—and who may even have been somewhat wilder than the artist himself had envisioned.

Alice was the Jacqueline Kennedy Onassis of her day: she had an innate sense of style and an aristocratic bearing that exuded self-confidence and inspired a generation of American women. At an early age, she had discovered the style that worked best for her and rarely wavered from it for the rest of her long life. Just as cartoonists had lampooned her father's famous toothy grin, caricaturists eventually targeted Alice's broad-brimmed hats, single-strand pearl necklaces, and shift-style dresses. Alice was the most copied and talked-about woman of the early twentieth century.

She was born in the Roosevelt family home on West Fifty-seventh Street in New York City on February 12, 1884. Her parents, Theodore Roosevelt and Alice Lee, young and wealthy and deeply devoted to one another, had been married less than four years. Roosevelt was beginning his political career as a New York State assemblyman in Albany and had moved his pregnant wife into his widowed mother's home in New York so that she would have company during her confinement. When news of the birth of his daughter reached him, he celebrated with his political cronies. A short while later, a second telegram arrived, urging him to return to New York at once. When he reached the family home at midnight on February 13, his brother Elliott met him at the door, wild with emotion: "There is a curse on this house! Mother is dying and Alice is dying too!" Roosevelt rushed upstairs to find his mother consumed by typhoid fever and his wife suffering from kidney failure. Both Alice and her mother-in-law died on Valentine's Day; a joint funeral was held two days later. On February 17, Teddy Roosevelt held his infant daughter as she was christened Alice Lee, in memory of her mother.

Roosevelt was overwhelmed by grief. He wrote in his diary, "When my heart's dearest died, the light went from my life forever." He left his daughter in the care of his unmarried sister Anna, known to the family as Bye, and returned to Albany. As soon as the legislative session ended, he resigned his post and traveled west to the Dakota Badlands, hoping the hard life of a cattle rancher would help him recover his spirits. He never mentioned his wife again and shied away from his only child, finding the memory of her birth too painful to bear.

Eventually, Roosevelt returned to New York, and despite his avowed disapproval of second marriages,

married a childhood friend, Edith Kermit Carow, in 1886. Although Teddy offered to leave Alice with his sister, Edith insisted on raising her husband's daughter. Alice moved with her father and stepmother to Sagamore Hill, the twenty-two-room Long Island home in which Teddy had intended to live with Alice Lee. Over the next eleven years, Teddy and Edith would have five children, and with the arrival of each new stepsibling Teddy's fatherly attentions grew more divided and Alice's behavior grew more unpredictable and rebellious. In her old age she would admit that she always felt like an outsider intruding on her father's second family.

Alice's parents insisted that their children receive an education appropriate to their status in society. Alice was schooled at home by a series of governesses, and during her teen years, when her parents decided to send her to a boarding school in New York, Alice threatened to humiliate the family if they made her go. Her parents relented, allowing Alice to educate herself in her father's expansive library. While she became extremely well read on a wide variety of subjects, the experiment left her undisciplined, and she remained a woman governed by her impulsive nature.

Teddy Roosevelt had inherited a sizeable fortune when his parents died, but lost the majority of it in a failed cattle ranch in the Dakota Territory. The money that remained had been spent on the construction of Sagamore Hill. While Edith struggled to make do with the salary Teddy earned as a politician, Alice received a regular allowance and extravagant gifts from her mother's parents. The Lees were an old, wealthy Boston family, and they lavished attention on Alice during the six weeks she spent with them each year. Alice's small income allowed her to be better dressed than her siblings. After visiting several well-established department stores on a shopping trip to New York, Edith wrote to her sister Emily, describing the lovely clothes she had bought Alice: "I got . . . a beautiful dress at Stern's, dark large plaid with navy blue velour . . . [which cost] forty-two dollars, and [a] coat [of] rough blue cloth lined throughout with plaid silk [which cost] forty-five dollars. Mrs. Lee wishes it, and I am glad as Alice is a child who needs good clothes."

As Alice blossomed into a beautiful young woman, she was eager to be treated as an adult. She yearned for long skirts and upswept hairdos instead of the childish dresses she was required to wear until her formal debut. While her father was governor of New York she was invited to be a bridesmaid in the wedding of her uncle George Lee. The youngest member of the wedding party, Alice, who was about sixteen years old at the time, was delighted that she would nonetheless be wearing a mature gown for the occasion. In her published memoir, *Crowded Hours*, she remembers the excitement: "How I loved that dress! I was sure that it made me look at least eighteen." Alice wore it at every opportunity in Albany until Edith determined that the gown was threadbare and should be given to the poor.

In 1900, Teddy Roosevelt was nominated to run for vice president with William McKinley on the Republican national ticket. McKinley defeated his Democratic opponent, William Jennings Bryan, and began his second term in the White House. At McKinley's inaugural ball, Alice wore a new dress of white *point d'esprit* that she absolutely hated because, she claimed, its juvenile style announced how young she was.

That September, McKinley was killed by an assassin's bullet and Roosevelt became the twenty-sixth

While Alice stands at the center of this 1903 photo, in reality she often felt like an outcast. She wrote in her diary: "Father doesn't care for me . . . one eighth as much as he does for the other children."

President of the United States. When he moved into the White House with Edith, it was the first time such a large family had occupied the executive mansion, and the American public loved reading about their exploits. Alice delighted in the attention from the press, and was happy to provide material for their subscribers to read about. As she later recalled in her memoirs, "I was the daughter of an enormously popular President, the first girl in the White House since the days of Nellie Grant, and I looked upon the world as my oyster. But my 'publicity value' was, I fear, at times a trial to the family." Indeed, Alice's family often deemed her behavior inappropriate and potentially damaging to the President. The papers were filled with stories, some true and some false, about her wild antics, which were said to include dancing at midnight on the rooftop of the Vanderbilts' Newport mansion, driving a car unchaperoned from Newport to Boston at the reckless speed of twenty-five miles per hour, and betting on horses at the racetracks.

By the age of seventeen, Alice had matured into a striking young woman. She was tall and lean with thick dark-blonde hair, a flawless complexion, and—her most captivating feature—large oval blue-gray eyes. She was, in short, the epitome of the spirited and athletic Gibson Girl, whose pompadour hairdo, starched blouses, and flared skirts represented the new American woman. Alice had the perfect figure to carry off the new fashions captured in the Charles Dana Gibson drawings. The hallmark of the Gibson-girl dress was the "S-bend silhouette," which owed its shape to a new type of corset that thrust the breasts forward and the hips back. On the delicate curve of the female form were draped sweeping trumpet-shaped skirts that were paired with lavish lace-and-ribbon-trimmed bodices and accompanied by broad-brimmed hats decorated with feathers. With her youth, beauty, and stylish wardrobe, Alice

The elaborate trims and rich fabrics of the Edwardian era could easily dwarf the wearer, but Alice's commanding personality and bearing stood up to the fashions of the day.

easily eclipsed First Lady Edith Roosevelt as the most popular and emulated woman in the country.

Four months after the Roosevelts moved into the executive mansion, Alice made her society debut. She was thrilled at the prospect of being the first daughter of a President to be introduced into society at a White House ball. As usual, Alice and her stepmother differed on what type of party to have. Alice wanted to serve champagne, as her wealthy friends had done at their debuts; Edith insisted upon fruit punch. Alice wanted to have elaborate favors for the guests; Edith forbade the extravagant expenditure. What Alice found most crass and humiliating was the floor. The East Room, where the party would be held, was carpeted; and since Edith Roosevelt's extensive restoration of the White House had not yet begun, a crude waxed linen floor cloth had to be put down for dancing. The night of the debut, Alice wore a white chiffon gown with rosebud appliqué, long white evening gloves, and a fashionable pompadour hairdo; she stood next to her stepmother as she was introduced to the six hundred invited guests. While Alice would later claim to have been bored by her debut, and disappointed yet again by the youthful gown she had to wear, her aunt Corinne Roosevelt Robinson noted that Alice "had the time of her life" with "men seven deep around her all the time."

U nderneath the sumptuous evening gowns and tailored sporting costumes of the early twentieth century, women wore a new type of corset with a long, lean, exaggerated line. This silhouette would come to define the fashion of the era, as worn by the Gibson Girl shown below.

Once she had been introduced into society, Alice embarked on a career in the spotlight, determined to set herself off from her family by breaking every convention in staid Washington society. She began by taking up smoking, and when her father forbade her to smoke in his house she simply went out on the White House roof instead. She socialized with a crowd of wealthy young people that included her new best friend, Marguerite Cassini, the daughter of the Russian ambassador (and later the mother of Oleg Cassini and gossip columnist Cholly Knickerbocker). Together, Alice and Marguerite dominated Washington society. "The younger set has a circle which is one of the most powerful and autocratic that has ruled social affairs since the days of Nellie Grant," wrote one newspaper columnist. "Miss Alice Roosevelt and Countess Cassini dominate this clique, and they possess absolute authority in admitting or refusing membership."

Teddy and Edith were losing patience with Alice's behavior. On one occasion, Alice repeatedly interrupted a meeting between her father and the American author Owen Wister. The third time she burst into the room, Roosevelt threatened, "Alice, the next time you come in, I'll throw you out the window." After Alice retreated, Wister looked at the President and asked him why he didn't rein in his oldest daughter. Roosevelt responded, "I can be President of the United States or I can attend Alice. I can't do both." Alice would admit thirty years later in her memoirs that "my major preoccupation was to 'have a good time,' and a good time meant to me consorting with people of my own age, total irresponsibility, and perpetual rushing from place to place, from one amusement to another with the curiosity of a puppy and as little sense of direction." In an effort to set herself apart from her siblings and to emphasize to her father just how late she had been staying out at night, Alice began rising at noon.

Alice's parents found it much easier to deal with their daughter by sending her on extended trips, and since Alice felt unwanted at the White House she happily complied. She became her father's unofficial goodwill ambassador, visiting Cuba and Puerto Rico, attending Mardi Gras in New Orleans, the Chicago Horse Show, and the Saint Louis World's Fair. While media reports emphasized the social aspects of Alice's trips, she was nonetheless a capable diplomat, successfully handling the tedium of endless receiving lines and other official government functions and showing she could be gracious and well mannered if she chose.

As Alice traveled around the country, the media followed, providing dispatches to a public eager to know everything about her life. Alice relished the attention. Her sophisticated style soon made her a fashion leader, despite her limited wardrobe. Even though the Lee family continued to provide Alice with an allowance, she frequently exceeded her monthly allotment by almost a thousand dollars as she struggled to keep up with her wealthier friends. She came to rely on her indulgent Grandfather Lee to bail her out on a regular basis. To make matters worse, reporters were constantly requesting information on what Alice would be wearing to public functions. To give the impression that she had an extensive wardrobe, Alice came up with a clever way of deceiving the press: she would provide Edith's social secretary with several different descriptions of a single dress; the secretary would in turn give these misleading descriptions to the media. The ruse worked, and the reporters never realized they were being fooled.

Two important elements of Alice's personal style emerged at this time: large portrait hats and "Alice blue" gowns. In the early years of the twentieth century, large hats adorned with ostrich feathers, flowers, or ribbons, reminiscent of those worn in portraits painted by the eighteenth-century English artist Thomas Gainsborough, became the fashion. While these hats tended to be quite large, designed as they were to provide proportional balance for the popular pompadour coiffure, Alice's hats were truly enormous, making her all the more noticeable in public. For her gowns she favored

Alice occasionally filled in as White House hostess, and after one triumphant event she was described as "very competent, thoughtful, picturesque, with an inexhaustible stock of pleasant surprises." She might have served at a reception similar to the one shown at right, held at the Roosevelt White House.

Opposite: *Reception at the White House* (detail), William Baxter Closson, 1908. Courtesy Sagamore Hill National Historical Site, NPS.

The Black Hat, Frank W. Benson, 1904. Museum of Art, Rhode Island School of Design.
Gift of Walter Callender, Henry D. Sharpe, Howard L. Clark, William Gammell, and Isaac C. Bates.

I n 1902, Alice was invited by Prince Henry of Germany to christen the kaiser's new yacht, which happened to be moored off the New Jersey coast. Teddy and Edith Roosevelt accompanied Alice to Jersey City, where Alice, wearing a blue velvet gown with a flared skirt and a high-necked, long-sleeved bodice, announced, "In the name of His Majesty the German emperor, I christen this yacht *Meteor*." As a token of his gratitude, the kaiser asked his brother to present Alice with a diamond-encrusted bracelet. Prince Henry and Alice were seen pleasantly conversing during the dinner that followed on the imperial yacht, and the press began to speculate that the prince might propose to Alice, despite the fact that he was already married. The conjecture of a possible royal romance earned Alice the moniker Princess Alice—a name that would follow her for the rest of her life.

In 1904, Teddy Roosevelt was elected President by what was then the largest margin in history. Alice was

a particular shade of blue that matched her blue-gray eyes. The color became known as Alice blue and was an immensely popular shade for women's dresses across the country. The phenomenon was even commemorated in the popular song "Alice Blue Gown." Although the color would eventually fall from public favor, it remained Alice's favorite.

delighted at the prospect of another four years in the White House. She thoroughly enjoyed the privileges of being the daughter of the President and the absence of any real responsibilities. On the day of the inauguration, she wore a white cashmere dress and coat, with an enormous white hat faced with black satin that she later described as being the size of a small wheel. The hat proved to be something of a problem, as she struggled to keep it on in the strong March winds. While watching the inaugural parade from the reviewing stand with the family, Teddy Roosevelt reprimanded Alice for waving to her friends. When she countered that he was doing the same thing, he bellowed, "But this is my inauguration!" On that day in particular, the President did not want his daughter stealing the limelight.

That evening, at the inaugural ball, Alice wore a beautiful gown of gold gauze with a white satin bodice and a long train scattered with pink roses. Unlike her ensemble at the inauguration four years earlier, this gown became one of Alice's favorites, and she eventually packed it away as a keepsake of her wonderful years in the White House.

In 1905, Teddy Roosevelt decided to send his secretary of war, William Howard Taft, on an inspection tour of the Far East. Alice was permitted to go along on what would be her first trip outside the country. Eighty people formed the official entourage, and Alice requested that Nicholas Longworth, a thirty-six-year-old Republican congressman from Ohio, be included. Alice had been competing with Marguerite Cassini for Nick's attention and thought the trip would be the perfect opportunity to win him over.

Alice brought an extensive wardrobe on the journey. As the daughter of the American President, she was going to be entertained lavishly by foreign governments and presented to Far Eastern royalty. She traveled with three large trunks, two sizeable hatboxes, a steamer trunk, many bags and boxes, and a special container for her sidesaddle. Because they would be touring the Far East in summer, Alice brought two-piece linen suits with blouses for day, embroidered linens and cottons for dressier occasions, such as afternoon garden parties, and the bridesmaid dresses with matching hats from the five weddings in which she had taken part. Added to these

The most photographed woman in the world during her father's presidency, Alice Roosevelt is pictured here wearing one of her trademark hats.

were dinner dresses, voluminous petticoats and other undergarments, plus riding habits, bathing suits, and tennis outfits. The breadth of Alice's wardrobe suggests the changing role of women and the impact these changes had on women's fashions. As women became more physically active in the 1890s, participating in various sports, including tennis and bicycling, appropriate clothing was required to meet the demands of these new activities. Each sport necessitated its own uniform, intended to provide the wearer with ease of movement and especially with a sense of propriety.

While sporting costumes helped pave the way for shorter skirts and other fashion reforms, their immediate impact was to augment the already large number of ensembles a fashionable woman needed in order to be appropriately dressed for luncheons, teas, dinners, receptions, balls, and theater outings. The popularity of cotton and linen fabrics meant that maintaining these clothes typically required the assistance of a lady's maid. Alice brought her personal maid, Anna, to keep her wardrobe in order and freshly pressed. Attempting to keep Alice's linen and cotton ensembles neat and wrinkle-free during the four-month tour became an exhausting effort for Anna, who had a nervous collapse during the trip and was sent to Manila for a rest cure by Secretary Taft.

Alice's popularity spread worldwide as reporters followed the entourage through the Far East, reporting on such events as Alice's presentation to the emperor of Japan and her audience with the dowager empress of China. She also continued to make front-page news with her unpredictable flights of fancy, such as learning the hula in Hawaii and jumping fully clothed into a makeshift pool on the deck of a ship. Years later, when she was teased by Bobby Kennedy about this famous incident, she still failed to see what all the fuss was about. Bathing suits of the period included a knee-length wool dress worn with dark stockings and bathing shoes; as far as Alice was concerned, wearing a bathing costume was almost the same as swimming with your clothes on. "Had I jumped into a swimming pool without my clothes," she told Kennedy, "that would have been outrageous." Taft, as Alice's chaperone on the trip, was often exasperated by the joie de vivre of his young charge.

During the trip, the romance between Alice and Nick Longworth deepened, and by the time they returned from Asia, they had agreed to marry. Although Alice had pursued Nick, she was having second thoughts and waited a month to tell her family of the engagement. With her parents' approval, plans were undertaken for a large formal wedding in the White House, to be held on Saturday, February 17, 1906. While Edith coped with the colossal task of planning the wedding, Alice basked in the attention the newspapers devoted to her upcoming nuptials. Even more to her liking were the gifts pouring in from all over the world. Foreign heads of state sent costly presents to the bride and groom, including fine silks and embroideries from China, a tapestry from France, a diamond-and-pearl pendant from Austria, and a large mosaic table from the king of Italy. Alice's favorite wedding present was a necklace of sixty-three matching pearls from the Republic of Cuba. Teddy Roosevelt was horrified by the ostentatious gifts and insisted that they be returned. Alice refused, so father and daughter worked out a compromise: Alice could keep all her wedding gifts as long as she wore a bridal gown of American manufacture. Alice agreed, but reluctantly,

The public's enormous interest in Alice Roosevelt's engagement to Congressman Nicholas Longworth spread as far as Europe, where the Illustrated London News *featured "Princely Gowns for a Republican Bride." The enormity of the event seems to have exhausted the bridal family, as shown in the photo above, taken immediately after the White House ceremony.*

as she had hoped to use one of the fine silks from China for her wedding attire.

The color and cut of Alice's wedding gown and trousseau were considered front-page news; on January 22, 1906, the *New York Sun* reported, "The rarity of White House weddings has put everyone on tip-toe with interest in the coming event. They have been equally interested in the wedding gown and other dresses in the trousseau. The marked individuality of Miss Roosevelt makes it certain that she could by no means leave either the material or the style . . . or the [embellishment] of the wedding trousseau to her dressmaker."

On the morning of the wedding, Alice made one last defiant gesture to aggravate her parents: with her wedding scheduled for twelve o'clock, Alice refused to rise before eleven. By that time, the grounds of the White House, which were always open to the public, were filled with spectators, souvenir hawkers, and food vendors. Alice had elected not to have any bridesmaids at her wedding, deciding that competing with her famous father—a man she claimed wanted to be "the bride at every wedding and the corpse at every funeral"—was going to be difficult enough.

As noon approached, Alice put on her wedding gown: white satin with a twelve-foot train of white and silver brocade that had been woven in the silk mills of Paterson, New Jersey. Lace that had adorned the wedding gown of her mother, Alice Lee, served as trimming. Alice incorporated two of her wedding presents into her attire—a diamond necklace that Nick gave her and the string of pearls from Cuba. As Edith had feared, Alice had not left herself enough time to prepare, and the bride was still struggling with her pompadour, which

Newspapers competed to provide their readers with the latest news on the White House wedding. Alice and her husband, Nick, were still hounded by photographers during their honeymoon in Cuba; the media frenzy that marred their nuptials was slow to subside.

kept collapsing under the weight of her full-length veil and wreath of orange blossoms, when the clock struck noon. Finally, a few minutes after twelve, the seven hundred guests watched Teddy Roosevelt escort Alice to the makeshift altar in the East Room.

After the wedding and reception, Alice and Nick departed for a honeymoon in Cuba, where they visited the scenes of her father's triumphs as a Rough Rider. Later that year they sailed to Europe, where they were presented to King Edward VII; Alice donned her wedding gown for the occasion. Subsequently, they were entertained once again by the kaiser on his yacht. Marital bliss proved elusive at times, as Nick bristled at being referred to as "Mr. Alice Roosevelt" and playing second fiddle to his famous wife.

When they returned to Washington, Alice made a concerted effort to become a good political wife, staying out of the limelight except when Nick wanted her by his side. She proved to be an excellent campaign partner, and with Alice's enormous popularity Nick easily won reelection to the House. Teddy Roosevelt was thrilled to discover how politically savvy Alice was, and wrote to one of his children, "[Alice] has more political sense than almost anyone I know, and I thoroughly enjoy talking matters over with her." Politics became the only way Alice and her father could communicate, and over time it drew them closer.

Alice's period as a conventional political wife didn't last long, however. As her marriage with Nick broke down, Alice threw herself into promoting her father's political agenda. Even after he left the White House in 1908, Alice continued to supply him with information and insight from the nation's capital. Politics was becoming Alice's passion, and her home in Washington was becoming the most influential salon in the city.

Alice's fame did not diminish after her father left the White House, and in the years leading up to World War I the styles she adopted helped introduce American women to the latest fashions from Europe. When French couturiers such as Paul Poiret advocated eliminating the corset and dressing in leaner lines, Alice happily complied. She shortened her skirts, discarded her corset, and shocked Washington society when she attended a ball wearing a dress of blue tulle that was short enough to provide a glimpse of her evening slippers, with their cut-glass heels, and even her ankles—a sight rarely seen in American social circles. And when Oriental designs began influencing Western dress, Alice brought out the silk pajamas she had purchased on her trip to China in 1905 and began wearing them in public. When criticized for adopting such a radical form of dress, Alice replied, "I urge all the ladies to wear [pants]. They're comfortable, economical, and save considerable cloth." Once again, Alice's plainspoken wisdom struck a resonant chord

Paul Poiret's corset-free Orientalist designs appealed to the thoroughly modern Alice.

with American women and helped to pave the way for a new style of dress—a straighter, more streamlined silhouette and shorter skirts—that would soon become the prevailing fashion.

In 1924, Alice Roosevelt Longworth took the country by surprise when she announced that after eighteen years of marriage she was pregnant with her first child. It was rumored that the child was a result of an extramarital affair. In February, Alice checked into Chicago's Lying-in Hospital. Her doctor, fearing the uproar that might follow if something went wrong during the birth, booked passage out of the country, just in case. On February 14, 1925, forty-two years to the day since her mother had died, Alice gave birth to a baby girl, whom she named Paulina. Her wit sharper than ever, Alice likened childbirth to "trying to push a grand piano through a transom." When she returned home to Washington, troops had to be called out to hold back the crowds that lined the streets from Union Station to the Longworth home to see Alice's infant daughter. After more than a quarter-century in the spotlight, Alice Roosevelt Longworth still captivated the American public.

In 1931, Nick Longworth died of pneumonia. A few years later, Alice and Paulina embarked on a trip to California, and stopped in Hollywood. Alice was entertained by every movie studio executive, and the stars, who as children had idolized Alice, asked to have their picture taken with her and shoved scraps of paper at her for her to autograph. "I grew up on the legend of Alice Roosevelt," the actress Helen Hayes recalled. "I can still see my family gathered around the kitchen table reading about her exploits. I was lost in admiration of her."

After Nick's death, Alice's influence in politics and fashion began to wane. On top of that, the favor long enjoyed by Alice's branch of the Roosevelt family was superseded when her distant cousin Franklin D. Roosevelt was elected President in 1932. She had always considered her Democratic cousin a political lightweight and was envious that he and his wife, Eleanor (Alice's first cousin), were moving into the White House. Alice had always hoped that Nick or her brother Ted might be elected President so that her family could return to the executive mansion in triumph.

Alice may have begun to disappear from the front pages, but during the last three decades of her life she became a Washington institution. No politician dared pass up a visit to Mrs. Longworth for fear they would become the next target of her razor-sharp wit. When Senator Joseph McCarthy, a man Alice disliked for his zeal in drumming out communists in the federal government, announced he was going to call her by her first name, Alice retorted, "My gardener may call me Alice, the trash man on my block may call me Alice, but you, Senator McCarthy, may call me Mrs. Longworth." No one, Republican or Democrat, was safe from Alice's caustic comments.

Before her death at age ninety-six, Alice noted that there was a resurgence of the wide-brimmed hats she had popularized in her youth. "I'm not as recognizable as I used to be," she told *The New York Times* in 1972. "Everyone's wearing hats these days. I look at my hat on so many heads. My good old hat. I think it's that attractive Bella Abzug who made them popular and I'm glad." To her last days, Alice remained a keen and highly engaged observer of both politics and fashion.

Alice Roosevelt Longworth's unconventional lifestyle and spirited personality encouraged a generation of women to express themselves freely in both their choice of words and mode of dress. Her sophisticated tastes set styles for American women for years, even after her father left the presidency. And while she would have been the first to admit that she did not fill her life with the history-book accomplishments of her cousin Eleanor, she enjoyed an unmatchable eighty-year reign as the unofficial doyenne of Washington society. The extent to which this remarkable woman permeated the national consciousness was perhaps most succinctly expressed by the English writer Dame Rebecca West, who noted in 1935, "Physically, [Washington] is dominated by the Washington Monument. Intellectually, spiritually, the city is dominated by the last good thing said by Alice Roosevelt Longworth."

In response to criticism from the media for her unorthodox behavior, Alice quipped: "The trouble with reporters is that they expect me to wear a halo and I only wear a hat."

Women
& P

3

Privilege of Rank

There has always existed among America's wealthy citizens a deep nostalgia, sometimes bordering on obsession, for the trappings, rituals, and prestige of European nobility. Flying in the face of the republican notions of equality and democratic social mobility, generations of women turned away from the ideals of the American Revolution in search of rank and privilege—and, more specifically, a titled European husband and all the elegance and finery such a marriage would bring. And when marriage into European nobility became difficult to attain, American high society created its own rigid social register.

In the years following the American Revolution, Elizabeth Patterson set herself apart as a sort of counterrevolutionary by marrying Jerome Bonaparte, the brother of the emperor Napoleon. She was the first prominent American woman to seek fame and fortune abroad by marrying into a European ruling family. But, as would be the case with so many other young women, her encounter with European royalty was tempestuous, falling far short of the romance she had anticipated.

As the young country grew, wealthy urban society began to develop its own social hierarchy, one based more on money than on inherited nobility. In the late-nineteenth-century economic boom that followed the Civil War, traditional New York society was besieged by wealthy social upstarts longing to be welcomed by the dowager empress of Fifth Avenue, Caroline Astor; she, along with her social advisor Ward McAllister, served as the official gatekeeper of East Coast society. Astor and McAllister had determined to limit New York society to four hundred people, the exact number of guests that Mrs. Astor's ballroom could comfortably hold. Their intent was to keep out the nouveau riche. To a wealthy woman with social pretensions, being snubbed by the Four Hundred was tantamount to being banished from New York's social elite.

In the 1870s, these social castoffs, following in the footsteps of Elizabeth Bonaparte, set out to find suitable, preferably titled, husbands in Europe for themselves or for their daughters. By and large, Europeans welcomed the well-to-do Americans. A prime example was the Prince of Wales, Albert Edward, who was the darling of fashionable London society. Frivolous and playful, he loved anything new and different and welcomed many young and attractive American girls into his social set. Wealthy mothers, eager to vindicate the snubs they had received in New York, shopped aggressively for a titled husband. Because many of Europe's old aristocratic families had fallen on hard times financially, the large dowries the Americans offered attracted many suitors.

Among the earliest of the American successes abroad was Jennie Jerome. Her socially aggressive mother, Clara, had failed to win acceptance in New York, but in London Jennie and her two sisters were very popular. Jennie became one of the first American women to marry into the English aristocracy when she wed Lord Randolph Churchill in 1876. She is better remembered today as the mother of Winston Churchill.

Another legendary match was the marriage in 1895 of Consuelo Vanderbilt and Charles Spencer-Churchill, ninth duke of Marlborough. Consuelo's mother, Alva, had succeeded in overthrowing Mrs. Astor as the doyenne of New York society. Encouraged by the number of young American women who had married into European aristocracy, Alva set her sights high and endeavored to win over the duke for her daughter, despite Consuelo's stout resistance. Not long after the lavish wedding, the duke discovered the benefits of having married the daughter of America's wealthiest family: it was Vanderbilt money that helped restore splendor to Blenheim Palace, the Marlborough family seat. Soon Consuelo became a favorite member of the Prince of Wales's social set. By 1906, however, the duke and duchess had separated, and in 1920 they divorced, prefiguring the fate of many similarly arranged marriages.

By the 1920s, acceptance of young Americans into the British aristocracy and other royal circles was somewhat curtailed. In 1937, when Baltimore-born Wallis Simpson married the heir to the English throne, the marriage brought King Edward VIII the pain of abdication and the scorn of his family and country. It would not be until the 1950s, when young Grace Kelly married the prince of Monaco, that American marriages to European royalty were once again in vogue.

Elizabeth Patterson Bonaparte

In the early nineteenth century, America was a country still attempting to establish a collective cultural identity. The majority of Americans embraced the principles of the American Revolution and supported the establishment of a republican form of government rather than a monarchy. In spite of the existence of a wealthy upper class, American society was already beginning to lionize the archetypal "self-made man," and indeed, the remarkable fluidity of the fledgling American society allowed many upstarts to succeed in the nation's social capitals. Elizabeth Patterson, the daughter of one of the wealthiest men in the United States, was apparently unmoved by the groundswell of egalitarian spirit that seemed to set the American social order apart from the old world European aristocracy. An extremely intelligent and ambitious woman, she intended to capitalize on her remarkable beauty, marry a man of aristocratic birth, and leave provincial Baltimore. At the age of eighteen, she appeared to have succeeded: she married Jerome Bonaparte, the youngest brother of Napoleon, and became the envy of women everywhere. And while her happiness was short-lived, her romantic alliance with a Bonaparte made her one of the era's best-known women, both in America and in Europe.

As the daughter of a wealthy merchant living in a major seaport, Betsy, as she was called, had the financial means to import French gowns and European fashion periodicals, allowing her to stay abreast of the latest styles. Young and daring, she was one of the few American women to embrace the classically inspired but sexually provocative French mode of dress, delighting in the way the sheer fabrics and low necklines revealed her

The artist Francois Joseph Kinson captured the beautiful thirty-two-year-old Elizabeth Patterson Bonaparte in 1817, as she endeavored to launch herself into European society.

attractive figure. And while many found her manner of dress unsettling, Betsy remained an unflappable proponent of the Empire style and was instrumental in opening the door to French fashions in early-nineteenth-century America. She inspired women to lay aside the heavy, figure-concealing fabrics, modest necklines, and full-cut skirts that disguised the body underneath. Betsy Patterson Bonaparte's ambitious pretensions to the French imperial family may have earned her fleeting notoriety, but her impeccable sense of style earned her a lasting reputation as one of the boldest fashion icons of her era.

William Patterson was a self-made man who had arrived in Philadelphia from Ireland in 1766 at the age of fourteen. Ambitious and shrewd, Patterson made his fortune during the American Revolution, importing ammunition from France for the American army. With his substantial earnings, he founded his own shipping business, and subsequently married Dorcas Spear, the daughter of a prominent Baltimore family. On November 6, 1785, their daughter Elizabeth was born. One of fourteen children, Betsy was a strong-willed child prone to emotional outbursts. William Patterson was

a stern disciplinarian who ruled his home like an autocrat. "I have always considered it a duty to my family to keep them as much as possible under my own eye," he once wrote, "so that I have seldom in my life left Baltimore, either on pleasure or business." The only real challenge to his authority came from Betsy, who chafed under his overbearing control.

By the time Betsy was eighteen, she was a ravishing beauty whose easy manners, vivacious personality, and quick mind made her the belle of Baltimore. She was extremely well read for her time, having studied, among other works, Mary Wollstonecraft's famous feminist treatise, *A Vindication of the Rights of Women*. It is fair to assume that this work—as it did with so many educated women of her era—had an enduring effect on Betsy's outlook on life, and indeed on the restrictive conventions of early American society.

In September of 1803, Betsy met Jerome Bonaparte, the nineteen-year-old brother of Napoleon. Jerome had been forced into the French

imperial navy by his older brother, who hoped that the rigor and discipline of a sailor's life would cure him of his pampered ways. At the end of a tour of duty in the Caribbean, Jerome took the liberty of sailing to the United States, seeking a holiday from the monotony of life aboard a naval vessel. He landed in Norfolk, Virginia, and proceeded up the coast to Philadelphia, where he would board a French ship bound for home. On his way he stopped in Baltimore, where he met Betsy at a ball. By all accounts it was love at first sight for Jerome, who was captivated by the petite, darkeyed brunette. By all outward appearances, Betsy was equally smitten by the young French lieutenant, though the prospect of marrying the brother of Napoleon, who ruled France as first consul, was no doubt a contributing factor in her sudden intoxication.

By October, Jerome had decided to marry Betsy and applied for a marriage license without William Patterson's permission. Furious at being circumvented, Betsy's father forbade her to see Jerome again and sent her to stay with relatives in Virginia. The headstrong Betsy was undeterred; she slipped out of Virginia and reunited with her lover in Baltimore, insisting that "she would rather be the wife of Jerome Bonaparte for an hour than married to any other man for life." (Little did she know how prophetic these words would be.) By this time, however, William Patterson had learned that under French law, Jerome, who was still a minor, could not legally marry without his parents' permission. Faced with this legal obstacle, Jerome supplied a copy of his naval commission, which erroneously listed

This detail of a cotton gown, worn by Betsy for her marriage to Jerome, captures the luxuriant simplicity of the fashions of the Empire period. Imported from India, fine cotton was the most novel and costly of fabrics. Its suppleness and fluidity helped to create the slim, delicate silhouette that characterized the Empire style.

his age as twenty-one. Seemingly deprived of further recourse, Betsy's father reluctantly gave his consent—with the stipulation that the young couple not leave for France until Napoleon had approved the marriage.

They were married on December 24, 1803, in the Patterson home. William Patterson, apparently reconciled with the prospect of being related to France's ruling family, endeavored to guarantee Napoleon's after-the-fact approval by having Betsy and Jerome married by the bishop and mayor of Baltimore, thereby making the marriage both legal in the United States and valid in the eyes of the Catholic Church. In a last effort to protect his daughter's interests, William Patterson had Jerome sign a prenuptial agreement promising Betsy one-third of her husband's estate if they separated for any reason.

For her wedding, Betsy wore a simple high-waisted gown of white Indian muslin, which draped in elegant folds, and a string of pearls at her neck. She later described her bridal garb as "a gown I had frequently worn, for I particularly wished to avoid vulgar display." A gentlemen guest at the wedding found even this simple wedding dress shocking. "All the clothes worn by the bride might have been put in my pocket," he noted. "Her dress was of muslin richly embroidered of extremely fine texture. Beneath her dress she wore but a single garment." Betsy was apparently adopting the French mode of dress, wherein a single chemise (a long, narrow slip), revealing the curves of the body, was worn beneath a gown, as opposed to the layers of undergarments that most American women wore out of modesty.

As a gift to his bride, Jerome had ordered Betsy a Parisian wardrobe consisting of gowns from Leroy, the renowned couturier to Napoleon's fashionable wife, Josephine. These gowns epitomized the new mode of dress inspired by the flowing garments depicted in ancient Greek sculpture. This new European style was rapidly replacing the prevailing fashions of the eighteenth century, which had concealed the body with rigid corsets and *paniers*, or hip-expanding hoops. Fashions from these early years of the French empire placed greater emphasis on the breasts, which were pushed up by a high waist and exposed by a low neckline and clinging fabric of fine cotton muslin. As the fabric fell in loose folds from the bustline, it revealed the curve of the wearer's hips and thighs, creating a remarkably unabashed—and, to many, risqué—sensuality.

Betsy yearned to socialize with the best of European society. This colored engraving from 1805, entitled Dancing Parisian Couples, *depicts the kind of company she longed to keep.*

The American public's reaction to the Patterson-Bonaparte wedding revealed an underlying fascination with the world of rank and privilege, and Jerome and Betsy basked in the attention. In the meantime, William Patterson dispatched his son Robert to France to personally inform the Bonapartes of the marriage and to engage the assistance of the American minister to France, Robert Livingston, in obtaining Napoleon's approval of the union.

Jerome and Betsy traveled to Washington for the winter social season, staying with her uncle, Robert Smith, who was secretary of the navy under President Thomas Jefferson. Soon after arriving, Betsy's scandalous fashions began to cause a stir in the new capital. Margaret Bayard Smith, wife of the publisher of the country's first national newspaper, the *Intelligencer*, wrote to a friend on January 23, 1804:

Mad'm [Bonaparte] . . . has made great noise here, and mobs of boys have crowded round her splendid equipage to see what I hope will not often be seen in this country, an almost naked woman. An elegant and select party was given to her by Mrs. Robt. Smith; her appearance was such that it threw all the company into confusion, and no one dar'd to look at her but by stealth; the window shutters being left open, a crowd assembled round the windows to get a good look at this beautiful little creature, for every one allows she is extremely beautiful. Her dress was the thinnest sarcenet and white crepe without the least stiffening in it, made without a single [pleat] in the skirt, the width at the bottom being made of gores; there was scarcely any waist to it and no sleeves; her back, her bosom, part of her waist and her arms were uncover'd and the rest of her form visible. [She was invited to another party the next evening] and several ladies sent her word if she wished to meet them there, she must promise to have more clothes on.

ELIZABETH PATTERSON BONAPARTE

The coronation of Napoleon signaled France's reemergence as the world leader in style and elegance. The classically inspired gowns worn by Josephine and her court, including Madame Recamier (above), fascinated American women, who considered them far too risqué to wear without modification.

Word of Betsy's scantily clad figure quickly spread through Washington and beyond. Simeon Baldwin, a member of Congress, wrote to his wife, "Young Bonaparte and his wife were here last week. I did not have an opportunity to inspect her charms, but her dress at a Ball which she attended has been the general topic of conversation in all circles. Having married a Parisian she assumed the mode of dress in which it is said the Ladies of Paris are clothed—if that may be called clothing which leaves half of the body naked and the shape of the rest perfectly visible . . . Tho' her taste and appearance was condemned by those who saw her, yet such fashions are astonishingly bewitching . . . we may well reflect on what we shall be when fashion shall remove all barriers from the chastity of women." Betsy's French fashions were new to many in the States, and although some older and more conservative Americans found them scandalous, they would become the prevailing style—in a more modest version—for the next fifteen years.

While Betsy and Jerome socialized in America, her brother Robert met in Paris with Jerome's older brother Lucien, who reported that "[my] mother, myself and the entire family unanimously and fully approve of the marriage. The Consul does not agree with us for the moment, but he must be considered the sole dissenting voice in the family." Napoleon was in fact furious that Jerome had married without consulting him; it was understood that his siblings were to reserve themselves for strategically important alliances with members of the European monarchies, and his dynastic ambitions were not going to be compromised by this American girl. In his eyes the marriage was null and void, since Jerome was a minor and had not received permission to wed.

In May of 1804, Napoleon proclaimed himself emperor of France, and the coronation ceremony was scheduled for December. Both Jerome and Betsy were anxious to return to France to take their rightful place in the imperial court. Several times they tried to sail for the Continent, but each time they were prevented from leaving by storms or the threat of attack from the British, who were at war with Napoleon. Finally, in March of 1805, Jerome and Betsy, who were expecting their first child, set sail for Lisbon aboard one of her father's ships. Once in France, Betsy planned to throw herself at Napoleon's feet, hoping her tears and beauty would win him over. When the couple reached Lisbon in April they were informed that the emperor had issued an order that prevented Betsy from landing at any port under French control. When the French ambassador asked Betsy if there was anything he could do to make her detention on ship more comfortable, she replied with characteristic bravado, "Tell your master that Madame Bonaparte is ambitious, and demands her rights as a member of the imperial family." While impressed with her verve, Napoleon was not moved to consent to the marriage.

Jerome left Betsy to meet with his brother and persuade him to accept his American wife. In the meantime, Betsy sailed for England, landing at Dover on May 19. Word had spread of the cruel manner in which Napoleon was treating his new sister-in-law, and a large crowd turned out to see the American woman who had upset the emperor's plans. A military escort had to be dispatched to protect Betsy from the crush of the mob. She settled into a house outside London to wait for the birth of her child and for Jerome to send for her. Jerome met with Napoleon, who informed him he must either give Betsy up or be disowned by the family. Having no income other than that which his brother provided, he agreed to abandon his wife. He was rewarded for his capitulation by being made a prince of the empire and an admiral in the French navy. Two years later, acceding to his brother's wishes, Jerome would marry Catherine, the daughter of the duke of Wurtemberg, and become king of Westphalia.

Betsy gave birth to a son, Jerome Napoleon Bonaparte, on July 7, 1805. She waited for good news from France, but by that autumn she recognized the hopelessness of her case and returned to Baltimore. The following March, an imperial decree declared her marriage null and void and all offspring illegitimate. In addition, Napoleon forbade her to use the name Bonaparte.

Devastated by her husband's rejection, Betsy moved back into her father's home. As the dazzling future she had planned for herself disappeared, she began to transfer all her hopes and aspirations to her infant son; through him she would attain the rank and privilege that Napoleon had denied her. She wrote the emperor, requesting financial support so that she could live independently and not be compelled to marry for economic reasons. Should she accept the hand of a wealthy Englishman, it might be embarrassing to the imperial family to have the nephew of the emperor raised by an enemy of France. Napoleon provided her with an annual pension of sixty thousand francs, which Betsy continued to receive until his abdication in April of 1816. She also requested Napoleon's permission to live in Paris with her son and asked that he provide her with an aristocratic title. General Turreau, the French minister in Washington, reported to Napoleon that Betsy "would like a name and a title without being obliged to marry—her ambition makes her more anxious for the éclat of rank than of money." Napoleon simply ignored this last request.

The dramatic, even epic, quality of Betsy's saga—filled as it is with equal measures of scandal, sex, diplomacy, court intrigue, and, of course, fashion—was not lost on the public. Her income from Napoleon allowed her to dress in the height of fashion, wearing provocative gowns and jewels that she felt were her prerogative as the wife of a prince of France. She was still considered one of the most beautiful women in the country, and her stunning ensembles drew praise. In February of 1812, Phoebe Morris, a young Quaker befriended by First Lady Dolley Madison, wrote to an acquaintance about her first meeting with Betsy: "How I wish you could see Madam Bonaparte in all the splendor

In her numerous sojourns abroad, Betsy delighted in the
best of European society and fashion. She embraced
the new romantic silhouette (pictured above),
characterized by nipped-in waistlines, full skirts, and
an abundance of rich, colorful trims.

of dress, and all the attractions of beauty. I think I never
beheld a human form so faultless. To the utmost symmetry
of features is added so much vivacity, such captivating
sweetness! And her sylphic form 'thinly veiled' displays
all the graces of a Venus de Medicis. She appears particularly lovely in a fine crepe robe of a beautiful azure
color interwoven with silver, in this attire she is truly
celestial, and it is impossible to look on anyone else when
she is present." The impact Betsy's high fashions had on
this young Quaker, and on hundreds of other women
raised in a tradition of more modest dress, was profound.
In an era when few American women wore gowns from
France, Betsy stood out. One of the few American women
to shine as brightly was Betsy's contemporary, Dolley
Madison, who also embraced French fashion and recognized the allure of a plunging neckline.

A born pragmatist, Betsy monitored her finances
personally, fearful that the allowance she received from
Napoleon would not be enough to provide adequately for
her and her son. Napoleon's exile in 1816 brought an
end to Betsy's stipend, but it also freed her from his
injunction on travel to Europe. She secured a divorce

from the Maryland legislature in order to protect her
small fortune from the spendthrift Jerome. Betsy
registered her son at Mount Saint Mary's College in
Emmitsburg, Maryland, and set sail for Europe, determined finally to take the Continent by storm.

Betsy was charmed by the
reception she received from the English aristocracy and
was delighted to socialize at long last with a class of people
she considered her peers. This trip, however, exacerbated
the mounting tension in her relationship with her father.
Claiming allegiance to the republican virtues espoused
by his adopted country, William Patterson was not
impressed with his daughter's social successes. He berated
her: "I hope and pray that you will perceive your mis-
take, and that you will look to your mother country as
the only place where you can be truly respected; for what
will the world think of a woman who . . . had quit her
father's house when duty and necessity called for her
attentions . . . and thought proper to seek admiration in
foreign countries?"

Betsy tried in vain to explain her actions to her
father: "I confess that it would perhaps have been a
blessing if I could have vegetated as the wife of some
respectable man in business; but you know that nature
never intended me for obscurity, and that with my dispo-
sition and character, I am better as I am . . . All my conduct is calculated. Let people think you are proud of me,
which in fact you have good reason to be, as I am very
prudent and virtuous."

Betsy basked in the attention she received in
Europe. Although it had been twelve years since her ill-
fated marriage, people were still fascinated with her
romantic interlude with a member of the imperial family. She so impressed the French statesman Talleyrand
that he astutely commented, "She married the wrong
brother"—recognizing that with her brilliance and beauty
she would have been a worthy consort for Napoleon.

Betsy returned to Baltimore in the summer of 1816,
and three years later she departed for Europe again, this
time bringing Bo, as the young Jerome was called. They
would spend the next three years in Europe, primarily in
Geneva, where Betsy could live inexpensively, provide

Bo with skilled tutors, and still enjoy European society. In a letter to his grandfather, Bo described his mother's lifestyle: "Mama goes out nearly every night to a party or a ball," he wrote. "She says she looks a full ten years younger than she is, and if she had not so large a son she could pass for five and twenty years old." Such reports from Europe could not have pleased her stern father, who felt her place was with him in Baltimore.

The collapse of the Napoleonic empire marked the beginning of a new era—one imbued with the new aesthetics of romanticism. In the social disarray left by the Napoleonic wars and the extravagance of the empire, fashion turned for inspiration to the purer days of monarchy that had dominated pre-revolutionary France. This redirection manifested itself in fuller skirts that emphasized the smallness of the waist, richer and heavier fabrics that rustled as a woman entered a room, and embellished hems and shoulders that projected a more delicate femininity. Remnants of the Empire style remained in the slightly raised waistlines and the short, full sleeves and low necklines for evening, but revealing fashions were on the decline.

In late 1821, Betsy and Bo were invited to spend the winter with members of the Bonaparte family, who had taken exile in Rome after Napoleon's abdication. Anxious to introduce Bo to his father's family and to win the acceptance she and her son had long been denied, Betsy accepted the invitation. They were warmly received by the family, who were startled by Bo's resemblance to the emperor, who had died earlier that year.

The family proposed to marry Bo to his cousin Charlotte; but her father, Joseph Bonaparte, one of the wealthiest members of the family, balked at Betsy's financial terms and the wedding negotiations fell through. Once again, the gulf between Betsy's expectations of the Bonapartes' largesse and their actual lack of generosity proved significant. After the engagement was broken off, she wrote to her father: "Nothing can or ever will surprise me in that family, there is no reliance to be placed on any of that race."

Bo returned to America in the spring of 1822 to prepare for his Harvard University entrance exams. When he graduated from the university in 1826, he sailed to Europe for his first meeting with his father, who was then living in Rome. Betsy, choosing not to live in the same city as her ex-husband, settled in Florence to be near her son. She relished the brilliant society there and the flattering attentions she received. She was admired for her exquisite gowns, which featured the enormous and popular gigot sleeves, nipped-in waists, and cone-shaped skirts, decorated in the most elaborate manner. These gowns, combined with her jeweled ornaments, created a bewitching image. Her admirers in Europe praised her youthful figure, which was likely maintained in part by the tight-laced corset that was considered a fashion necessity.

"Florence is much more agreeable than Paris, and indeed I never had as many invitations as I have had here," Betsy wrote her father in 1827. As usual, he could show only displeasure for her lifestyle. She responded angrily to his criticisms: "I think it is quite as rational to go to balls and dinners as to get children, which people must do in Baltimore to kill time." As Betsy grew more resentful of her father's reprimands, her responses included more and more assaults upon the institution of marriage and what she deemed the foolish practice of Americans marrying for love rather than wealth or rank. Her cynical view of romantic love began to taint her plans for Bo's future. She admonished her son about the importance of marrying a woman who was his equal in rank, warning against the impropriety of marrying or settling in America.

In 1827, Bo returned to America, but Betsy did not go with him because she was having such a wonderful time in Italy. While living in Baltimore with his grandfather, Bo fell in love with Susan May Williams, a young woman from a wealthy Baltimore family. William Patterson encouraged his grandson in his courtship and wrote Betsy when Bo and Susan became engaged. Betsy was furious that her son would marry an untitled American, and felt deeply betrayed by her father, who had helped arrange a match of which he knew she would disapprove.

Bo and Susan were married by the archbishop of Baltimore on November 3, 1829, at the Williams home on North Charles Street. Betsy wrote from Europe, "I feel that I have no right to make another person adopt my standard of happiness. I would rather die than marry any one in Baltimore, but if my son does not feel as I do upon this subject, of course he is quite at liberty to act as he likes best."

Bo's marriage, and his rejection of the lifestyle Betsy had planned for him, left her completely devastated. Depressed and resentful, she informed her son that she would no longer provide him with an allowance, and that he was no longer the beneficiary of her estate. She requested that all her jewels, laces, and gowns remaining in Baltimore be sent to her at once. While she had never skimped on her wardrobe, she now spent even more lavishly. By this time, fashionable women's dress had taken on literally enormous proportions, as seen in what were then called "imbecile" sleeves, held out by down-filled cushions worn on the arm, and in the full skirts supported by numerous layers of petticoats. She also set out to have her collection of jewels reworked and placed in more stylish settings. "I have had all my emeralds and diamonds, with twenty large pearls and three white topazes," she wrote to an acquaintance, "made into a magnificent ornament for my head. My solitaire diamond ring and a solitaire which I took out of a pin [that once belonged to Princess Borghese, her former sister-in-law] I have had added to my earrings. My turquoise ring, my diamond garter ring, my emerald ring, my emerald cross, and two pairs of emerald earrings, are all in the head ornament. It is so contrived as to serve for the head, the neck and the waist—the three white topazes are to be mistaken for diamonds."

While plans for her wardrobe proved an amusing distraction, they could not hide the fact that she was lonely. At the age of forty-four, Betsy was tired of the criticism from her family for living independently and socializing with Europe's idle elite. The joyous woman she had been in her youth had been replaced by an increasingly bitter one, who used her biting wit to strike at anyone who mocked her. "Everything in this world tires me," she confided to her closest friend, the English writer Lady Sydney Morgan. "I don't know why, unless it be the recollection of what I have suffered. I am of your opinion: the best thing a woman can do is to marry; even quarrels with one's husband are preferable to the ennui of a solitary existence."

After nine years abroad, Betsy prepared to return to Baltimore in the summer of 1834. Before leaving Europe, she went on a buying spree, acquiring enough gowns, accessories, and other finery to last her a number of years. Upon her return, she found that the few friends she had were either dead, living elsewhere, or estranged from her. She rarely went out, but when she did she most often wore what became her usual style in her later years: a full-skirted black velvet dress with a low neckline, short full sleeves, and one of her magnificent diamond necklaces.

Later that year, Betsy's father died. His will, written in 1827, was yet another indictment, materially and emotionally. "The conduct of my daughter Betsey [sic]," it read, "has through life been so disobedient that in no instance has she ever consulted my opinions or feelings; indeed, she has caused me more anxiety and trouble than all my other children put together, and her folly and misconduct have occasioned me a train of expense that first and last has cost me much money. Under such circumstances it would not be reasonable, just, or proper that she should inherit and participate in an equal portion with my other children." Betsy inherited the comparatively small bequest of eight properties in Baltimore. Due to her shrewd business management, these possessions became very valuable, greatly increasing her wealth.

In 1860, Jerome Bonaparte died, leaving a will that made no mention of his first wife or their son. Betsy saw this as her last opportunity to attain the recognition she and Bo had long been denied. They sued Jerome's estate, stating that Bo, as Jerome's firstborn son, was entitled to his equitable share in the estate. There was no financial benefit to come from the suit, however, since Jerome, who always lived beyond his means, had died nearly bankrupt. It was Betsy's intent simply to prove that the marriage had been legally valid. The trial attracted wide interest in America and Europe and garnered sympathy for Betsy and Bo, and the court found merit in their arguments. But to acknowledge a line of American Bonapartes would have caused confusion in the succession of the imperial line—something that was unspeakable in the eyes of the court, which was answerable once again to a Bonaparte: Bo's first cousin Napoleon III, who had recently assumed power.

Betsy then retired to Baltimore, distancing herself from her family and friends by living in a boarding house. Her room was piled high with trunks filled with clothing and jewels—possessions that told the story of her remarkable life. Occasionally, she would display her old gowns for visitors. Among the items she had saved were her bridal gown and the suit Jerome had worn on their wedding day. She continued to monitor her investments closely, accruing an estate worth one and a half million dollars. Her annual income from this sum was one hundred thousand dollars, but she lived frugally on two thousand dollars a year. "Once I had everything but money," she said. "Now I have nothing but money."

She died on April 4, 1879, at the age of ninety-four, surviving her only child by nine years. A private funeral was held at the home of her daughter-in-law for the small group of family and friends who came to pay their last respects. During her long life, Betsy had refused to compromise her aspirations and conform to society's expectations. In so doing, she became a woman of independent spirit and means whose personal style brought her fame and adulation, making her a fashion leader both here and abroad. She can be credited with helping to introduce Americans to a revolutionary new style of dress in the early nineteenth century. As she rarely failed to point out in her letters, her life was of her own making. She wrote her father in 1827: "It has required the utmost exertion of the capacity and prudence which God gave me to make anything out of the hard fate which was allotted me. I am one of the few persons in the world who owe their position in society to their own efforts, and, really considering everything, I have some merit in having worked my way to the consideration and respect which are shown me both in America and Europe." Indeed, Elizabeth Patterson Bonaparte, like so many trendsetting women who followed her, quickly learned that if loneliness is the price you pay for bucking social conventions, the esteem and appreciation of future generations is the reward.

American artist Gilbert Stuart captured the beauty of Elizabeth Patterson Bonaparte in this interesting study for a portrait. Late in her life, Betsy reflected on her marriage: "Had I waited with my beauty and wit, I would have married an English duke, instead of which I married a Corsican blackguard."

Wallis Warfield Spencer Simpson

A young Prince of Wales appears in the photo above. In this portrait at left, Wallis assumes a languid, aristocratic pose. Consumed by her desire to present a regal appearance to society, she hid her plebeian beginnings behind one of the finest haute couture wardrobes of the twentieth century.

In 1936, a crisis shook the British establishment to its core, setting off an unprecedented media frenzy on both sides of the Atlantic. At the heart of the commotion was a plain-looking, forty-year-old, twice-married Baltimore native who had captured the heart of a handsome prince—the soon-to-be-crowned King Edward VIII—who would, famously, abdicate the throne rather than be separated from the woman he loved. Her name was Wallis Simpson, and in the eyes of countless American women, her story was mesmerizing. Here was a middle-class woman who wooed an English monarch and whose international popular appeal rivaled that of Hollywood's biggest screen idols.

Born into a destitute but once-prominent Baltimore family, Wallis Warfield rose above her impoverished upbringing by creating around herself an aura of gentility. She understood the power of clothes and throughout her life would carefully construct a wardrobe that would further her social ambitions. Her style was the epitome of 1930s chic: for day, beautifully tailored suits consisting of narrow jackets and slim skirts that fit smoothly over her narrow, boyish hips; and for night, sleek evening gowns that served as a backdrop for her extraordinary collection of jewels. And while it took years for her style to evolve, by the time she became a celebrity her look was being imitated all over America. "Everyone wanted to copy her," observed French couturier Hubert de Givenchy. "Even women who didn't have her figure or style wanted to dress as she did."

Her parents were descended from prominent Southern families, but despite their connections they were almost penniless when their only daughter was born on June 19, 1896. She was named Bessiewallis after her father, Teackle Wallis Warfield, who died of tuberculosis while she was still an infant. With no means of financial support, Wallis and her mother, Alice Montague Warfield, lived with various family members in Baltimore, including Wallis's beloved aunt, Bessie Merryman. Shuttled among the homes of her wealthy relatives, Wallis grew up with the stigma of being the poor ward of the family. Alice scraped together enough money to send her daughter to a private school for girls, but the experience was trying for young Wallis, who was ashamed of her homemade dresses and darned stockings. Childhood acquaintances would remember that, despite her limited wardrobe, Wallis was fastidious about her appearance; her clothes were always immaculate and she was perfectly groomed.

The poor relation of a socially prominent Baltimore family, Wallis hoped that her debut in 1914 would propel her into the coveted world of wealth and prestige.

In 1914, with financial support from her family, Wallis made her official society debut. Out of five hundred young women, she was among the forty-eight chosen to be presented at Baltimore's Bachelor Cotillion. Since she couldn't afford to buy a dress at one of the fashionable stores in town, she hired a dressmaker to copy a Worth gown of white satin with a white chiffon knee-length tunic trimmed in pearls. Wallis recognized at an early age that by choosing the most flattering fashions and eye-catching details she could garner the attention she desperately wanted. She did not become a slave to fashion trends, and she recognized the importance of wearing clothes that set off her best features. She also knew that the creation of a personal style would take time.

Soon after her debut, Wallis visited her cousin Corinne Mustin, who was living with her husband at the naval air station in Pensacola, Florida. There Wallis met a pilot, eight years her senior, named Earl Winfield Spencer, Jr. Aviation was still in its infancy, and Wallis was swept off her feet by the dashing young flyer. They married in November of 1916. At her wedding, Wallis wore a gown of white panne velvet with a long train and a tulle veil secured by a coronet of orange blossoms. She designed her bridesmaids' ensembles, selecting orchid faille for the full-skirted dresses, which were embellished by wide blue velvet sashes and coordinating hats.

From the outset, the marriage was troubled. Spencer was a violent alcoholic who made his new wife the object of his aggressions. After five years, Wallis, who intended to divorce Spencer, was persuaded by her family to settle for separation rather than disgrace the family name with a divorce. Three years later, Spencer, by then stationed in Hong Kong, pleaded with Wallis for a second chance. Shortly after their reconciliation, however, Spencer's old patterns returned, and in 1925 Wallis returned home and filed for divorce.

In 1926, Mary Kirk Raffray, a friend from Wallis's school days in Baltimore, invited Wallis to visit her and her husband in New York. There, Wallis met their friend Ernest Simpson, the English-born son of a successful shipping broker. Wallis and Simpson got along well, and over the next year a friendship developed. When Simpson was called back to England, he asked the newly divorced

Wallis to marry him. Wallis was filled with doubts: she didn't love Simpson, yet thought he would provide her with the financial security and stability she had never known. In July of 1928, she wrote to her mother, "I've decided definitely that the best and wisest thing for me to do is to marry Ernest. I am very fond of him and he is kind, which will be a contrast . . . I'm sure I shall be lonely next winter and homesick. However, I can't go on wandering for the rest of my life and I really feel so tired fighting the world alone and with no money." On July 21, 1928, they were wed in London's Chelsea Registry office.

The Simpsons rented a flat in a fashionable London neighborhood and Wallis began to decorate their home. She had a good eye for color and room arrangements, but what she truly excelled at was household management. Distancing herself from the memory of her own chaotic upbringing, Wallis ran a smooth and efficient household, developing a reputation as a skilled hostess among a close circle of friends. Wallis became friendly with Connie Thaw, who was the wife of the first secretary at the American embassy and one of the famous Morgan sisters. Her sister Gloria was the wife of Reggie Vanderbilt, and Gloria's twin, Thelma, was married to Viscount Furness; Thelma was also the Prince of Wales's latest mistress.

Maintaining a wardrobe fit for the social scene of her prominent friends was a constant challenge for Wallis. Relying on the thrift and ingenuity she had acquired as a young woman in Baltimore, she managed to expand her limited wardrobe, selecting clothes that could be easily remade, or at least refreshed with new trim or other embellishments. She also began consigning her clothes to increase her clothing allowance.

After years of stagnation following World War I, French designers were once again spearheading fashion trends for women in Europe and America. In the 1920s,

During the 1920s, as Wallis used her limited means to create an imaginative wardrobe, a change was occurring across the English Channel. In the fashion houses of Paris, the French couture industry was beginning to enjoy a resurgence. Designs by Madeleine Vionnet are pictured here.

Coco Chanel revolutionized women's fashion with the utter simplicity of her jersey separates. By the early 1930s, Madeleine Vionnet introduced the bias cut, which manipulated the natural drape of a fabric so that it clung to the body and moved gracefully with the wearer, creating the most close-fitting garments ever to appear in Western dress.

In 1930, when Wallis came into a small inheritance from an uncle, she took a trip to Paris, where she selected a few good couture pieces for her wardrobe. As she would later write in her memoirs, "The prospect of at last having a few chic clothes from the great couturiers

was more than I could resist." The outfits purchased from the English-born designer Molyneux, who specialized in dresses of pure simplicity that were devoid of any excess ornamentation, helped boost Wallis's self-confidence in her new life in England. "Molyneux," wrote Caroline Rennolds Milbank in her book *Couture*, "was the designer to whom a fashionable woman would turn if she wanted to be absolutely 'right' without being utterly predictable in the twenties and thirties." Dressed conservatively, but with aristocratic elegance, Wallis was finally beginning to develop her style.

In January of 1931, Thelma Furness and the Prince of Wales planned to spend the weekend together at her country retreat, with her sister Connie Thaw serving as chaperone. When Connie's mother-in-law became ill, she asked Wallis to take her place. Wallis, who was suffering from a bad cold, was taken aback by the request and was filled with trepidation at meeting the prince. Nevertheless, on Saturday, January 10, Mrs. Wallis Simpson met Edward, Prince of Wales, heir to the English throne. The prince, or David, as he was known to his family and friends, was thirty-six years old, blonde, and blue-eyed, with a graceful, athletic build. He loved any form of pleasure that distracted him from his more tedious royal duties; he was well known for his extravagant lifestyle.

Flush from a few days of successful mingling with the prince's exclusive group of friends, Wallis arranged

to be presented at court, thus securing her official introduction to English society. Borrowing a sleeveless white satin bias-cut gown, a white satin embroidered train, and a feathered headpiece and fan from Thelma and Connie, Wallis sought to make her appearance unique by purchasing a necklace of faux jewels. She described the piece in a letter to Aunt Bessie: "I am buying an aquamarine and crystal ornament and large aquamarine cross to wear around the neck which hangs center front of bust—really lovely on a white dress. These I need not add are imitations but effective." The large cross made a dramatic contrast against the stark simplicity of the dress and is an indication of what would become typical of her style—clean, streamlined evening gowns that set off her remarkable collection of real jewels. After their presentation at court, Wallis and Ernest Simpson attended a party hosted by Thelma Furness, where they again met the prince.

Over the next several years, as Wallis and Thelma became close friends, the Simpsons saw a great deal of the prince, both at his home, Fort Belvedere, and at their London flat. The prince, who was fascinated by Americans, delighted in Wallis's exuberance and outspokenness. In 1934, Thelma left for an extended trip to the States to assist her sister, Gloria Vanderbilt, who was facing a custody lawsuit brought by her sister-in-law, Gertrude Vanderbilt Whitney. Before Thelma left, she asked Wallis to "look after" the prince while she was away. The prince leaned on the women in his life, and with Thelma away he turned to Wallis for comfort and encouragement. "We have inherited the 'young man' from Thelma," Wallis wrote Aunt Bessie. "He misses her so that he is always calling up and the result is one late night after another—and by late I mean four a.m. Ernest has cried off a few but I have had to go on. I am sure the gossip will now be that I am his latest. It's all gossip about the Prince. I'm not in the habit of taking my girlfriend's beaux . . . I think I amuse him . . . and we like to dance together—but I always have Ernest hanging around my neck so all is safe." Wallis and Ernest were apparently settling into an arrangement common among the prince's circle: while her husband looked the other way, immersing himself in his business affairs, Wallis kept pace with the vacuous and permissive lifestyle at Fort Belvedere.

When Thelma returned, she was shocked to see that she had been effectively replaced by Wallis as the object of the prince's affection. Although Wallis tried to assure her friend that there was no affair, Thelma chose to break off her relationship with the prince. And indeed, what began as a sort of affectionate dependence on the part of the prince appeared to be developing into something more passionate; still, Wallis was sure that she

would be a temporary fling until someone younger and more amusing came along. As the relationship between Wallis and the prince became more serious, he began to shower her with jewels and provide her with money to buy fine clothes. On one occasion, she wrote to Aunt Bessie, "I bought a coat and dress with the $200 the Prince gave me and some leopard skins which I think will make a lovely sports coat."

The American decorator and arbiter of taste Elsie De Wolfe—later known as Lady Mendl—became Wallis's mentor, introducing her to the couturiers whose designs best suited her slim, angular body. Wallis began buying the sleek, sophisticated day dresses and evening gowns designed by Mainbocher and the surrealist-inspired designs of Elsa Schiaparelli.

Mainbocher created ensembles imbued with a sense of propriety and restraint that, in the words of former *Life* magazine fashion editor Sally Kirkland, "not only made a woman look like a lady, but as if her mother had been a lady too." This approach to women's clothing appealed to Wallis's need to conceal her humble origins and create an aura of cultured sophistication. The Italian-born Elsa Schiaparelli, on the other hand, appealed to Wallis's sense of fun. Schiaparelli had the uncanny ability of blending fashion with modern art, going so far as to hire Salvador Dali and other surrealist artists to design

English society photographer Cecil Beaton, who photographed Wallis in one of her Schiaparelli gowns (left), said of her: "Her taste in clothes shows always a preference for bold simplicity. Her hair, like a Japanese lady's hair, is brushed so that a fly would slip off it."

fabrics for her collections. By the end of the 1930s, she had become one of Paris's most popular couturiers.

Under the tutelage of these masters of design, Wallis learned to accentuate her slim figure rather than camouflage it with artificial curves. For day, she embraced a pared-down style that eschewed superfluous decoration. Her naturally lean lines were well suited to the fashionable silhouette of the 1930s: body-hugging, bias-cut fabrics, fitted sleeves, and tapered skirts that flared at the hem. This new style required new undergarments that would not be visible through the popular crepe and silk dress fabrics. Bras that lifted and supported the bust and small silk panties were a dramatic departure from the torso-encumbering corsets, cotton drawers, and petticoats of thirty years earlier. The restrictive garment of choice in a woman's wardrobe during the 1930s was the girdle, which helped full-bodied women maintain a smooth appearance in the figure-revealing fashions. By 1935, Wallis's sophisticated couture ensembles and minimalist fashions earned her the recognition of a number of Paris designers, who placed her on their best-dressed list for the first time.

Wallis described her life as the prince's companion as "Wallis in Wonderland." She lived for the moment, sure that at any time the prince would replace her with another woman who would become his wife. Late in 1935, she wrote to Aunt Bessie of the amazing life she was leading and reflected on her more humble roots: "I enjoy meeting all these people and sometimes it seems strange to think of the days of struggle in . . . the [Baltimore] flat where mother . . . was forever working herself to death to give me things. I wonder if in any way I'll ever be able to reward her efforts? Or if my insatiable ambitions will land me back in a one-room flat on Connecticut Hill [in Washington]?" Ernest Simpson didn't appear to object to his wife spending time with

the Prince of Wales. For her part, Wallis was careful to maintain the dignity of her marital relationship, so that she might return to that security when the prince tired of her.

In January of 1935, the prince's father, King George V, died. The moment the prince had been dreading his entire life had arrived. He felt overwhelmed by the responsibility and was unwilling to carry on as king without Wallis by his side. Several weeks after ascending to the throne, he began to intimate to Wallis that he wanted to marry her, and Wallis did everything in her power to dissuade him. Finally, the king approached Ernest Simpson, who agreed to provide Wallis with grounds for divorce. He, too, had been having an affair—with Wallis's school chum Mary Raffray, the very woman who had introduced the Simpsons to one another nine years earlier. While Wallis was furious that plans had been made without consulting her, she realized that a return to life as it had been would be impossible.

That summer, the king and Wallis cruised the Dalmatian coast of Yugoslavia with friends. American reporters followed them throughout their vacation, and when Wallis retreated to Paris at the conclusion of the trip she was horrified to discover that stories of her relationship with the king were splashed across the front pages of newspapers in the United States. The articles openly speculated on her divorce from Simpson and her impending marriage to the king. Only then did Wallis realize the catastrophe that loomed before her. She immediately wrote the king, suggesting that they break off their relationship and that she return to Simpson. But the king refused to consider her proposal, and indicated he was ready to give up the throne for her. Wallis felt trapped; she couldn't convince the king to stop the plans he had already set in motion. She also saw that all the social successes she had enjoyed in England were about to crumble at her feet, since she would no doubt be blamed for the king's decision. During the mounting political turmoil, the British press kept the story out of the papers in deference to the private life of the monarch; this abdication crisis was the last time the English press would afford the royal family such a courtesy. The resolve of British propriety was such that even American papers carrying reports of Wallis Simpson's divorce hearing were ordered removed from the newspaper stands in London. That same month, the king gave Wallis an engagement ring—a large deep-green emerald in a platinum setting from Cartier that had cost him ten thousand pounds.

In early December, as the English papers were finally about to run the story of the king's love affair and possible abdication, Wallis fled to France. Several days later, she released a statement offering to leave the king so he could fulfill his royal obligation.

On December 10, 1936, in a radio address to the nation, King Edward VIII abdicated his throne; in his speech he uttered the immortal words that today seem the stuff of fairy tales: "[it is] impossible to do my duty as King and Emperor without the help and support of the woman I love." In France, Wallis listened to the address and became hysterical. How could she ever repay a man who gave up his throne and his country for her? The newly dubbed Duke of Windsor left to join Wallis in Europe.

While the British public despised Wallis (though she commanded enough interest to have her likeness included in Madame Tussaud's wax museum), American women were captivated by her. The romantic circumstances of her life fascinated middle-class women whose own lives were bound to the daily routines of housekeeping and child-rearing in an economy still recovering from the effects of the Great Depression. Women were content to overlook the fact

that Wallis was an adulteress soon to be divorced a second time. What seemed to matter most was that she was like them, an ordinary woman from a modest background, and she was about to embark on an extraordinary life. As *Life* magazine noted shortly before the wedding, "Women of the world were little absorbed in the conventional satin gowns of England's new Queen. What Mrs. Wallis Warfield Simpson would wear, however, roused their avid curiosity."

American newspapers carried details of Wallis's life of exile in France and of her plans for her wedding and bridal trousseau. She ordered sixty-six outfits, including pieces from Mainbocher, Schiaparelli, Molyneux, and Pacquin, plus accessories such as hats, gloves, shoes,

On her wedding day (above), Wallis wore a gown created exclusively for her by Mainbocher. The photograph on the left shows women working on the wedding gown in Mainbocher's atelier; the dress was copied as a McCall's pattern (next page).

123

handbags, and, of course, jewels. Among the outfits she selected was Schiaparelli's famous lobster dress, a white organza evening gown that displayed on its skirt Salvador Dali's image of a red lobster surrounded by sprigs of parsley. Another Schiaparelli evening ensemble consisted of a floor-length coat of navy-blue horsehair net that fastened in the front with butterfly-shaped buttons and was worn with a plain blue crepe sheath underneath.

In early March, *The New York Times* reported that at a recent convention of beauticians, Wallis Simpson was praised for the stylish example she set for young women: "Mrs. Wallis Simpson has been a good influence in raising the standards of American beauty." It was anticipated that Wallis's coiffure—hair parted in the middle, smoothed in waves on either side, and drawn back into a small, neat chignon—would soon be the rage.

As the June 3 wedding date approached, Americans responded enthusiastically to the prospect of one of their own marrying the former king of England. Excitement soon swelled into cult-like fascination: in Baltimore, for example, a group of citizens purchased the house Wallis had grown up in and opened it as a museum, complete with dioramas depicting scenes from Wallis Simpson's life, including her days with the prince at Fort Belvedere and her presentation at court. It also featured a mural that, according to an editorial in *The New York Times*, showed "Mrs. Simpson and the Duke of Windsor in classical robes supporting heavenly constellations in their hands. The painted Duke remarks: 'I find it an impossible burden without the woman I love.'" The exhibit was a huge success.

Shortly before the wedding, the duke and Wallis received news that the royal family would be boycotting the upcoming nuptials and that Wallis would be denied the title Her Royal Highness. Wallis had anticipated this reaction; she understood that she and her husband would be shunned by the royal family for the damage they had inflicted upon the monarchy. But the duke was stunned by the venomous anger

Cecil Beaton photographed the future Duchess of Windsor in the famous Schiaparelli lobster evening gown.

directed at him and his fiancée. He would never forgive his family for this snub to his wife.

They were married on June 3, 1937, in front of a makeshift altar in the music room of the Château de Candé in France. Wallis wore a simple gown designed for the occasion by Mainbocher. The gown of silk crepe was "Wallis blue," a shade of medium blue that was a favorite of the bride. It featured a fitted jacket with long sleeves, a high neckline with vertical gathers above the heart-shaped bust and a long skirt that fit smoothly over the hips and flared at the feet. Wallis wore a hat of blue straw by Caroline Reboux of Paris that framed her face and was decorated with blue and pink feathers. Her matching blue crepe gloves had a slit cut in the ring finger of the left hand to accommodate the wedding band of Welsh gold. While the wedding ensemble received mixed reviews, it was a suitable gown for a woman entering her third marriage, and its simple elegance was appropriate for the wedding of a former king. It became the most copied dress of 1937 and influenced that season's fall fashions. Manufacturers rushed to produce dresses in "Wallis blue" that featured high necks, high waists, and narrow skirts. After the wedding, a six-page layout, photographed by Cecil Beaton and featuring

*No detail was too small for Wallis's scrutiny—
including those on customized accessories such
as handbags bearing her royal monogram
and a tiger-handled lorgnette.*

Wallis in some of her trousseau gowns by Mainbocher and Schiaparelli, appeared in the American edition of *Vogue* magazine. The issue sold out immediately.

Armed with her large supply of haute couture fashions, Wallis, now the Duchess of Windsor, set out to create a kingly exile for the duke. Wallis believed she owed her husband an enormous debt for the sacrifice he had made for her. "My husband gave up everything for me," she told society columnist Elsa Maxwell. "I'm not a beautiful woman. I'm nothing to look at, so the only thing I can do is dress better than anyone else. If everyone looks at me when I enter a room, my husband can feel proud of me. That's my chief responsibility." Wallis was determined to become the best-dressed woman in the world. As she worked with Paris designers in creating a look that captured the essence of her style, she in turn influenced American women, who looked to her as the epitome of the modern sophisticate. While she would never be queen of England, she would convince the world that, by dressing the part, she could be a suitable consort for a king. In public and private, her appearance was always immaculate. She could not stand to have a single strand of hair out of place, and according to one of her hairdressers she had her hair redone as often as three times a day. She insisted on working with her designers on the ensembles she purchased in order to assure that they fit her slender figure perfectly; often she would have nonessential decorative details removed. Once she had developed a wardrobe that suited her, Wallis became extremely disciplined about fitting into it, restricting her diet so she could maintain her 34-25-34 figure.

Every detail of her wardrobe and each shopping trip was reported in the American press. When, in October of 1937, Wallis's latest order of clothes turned out to be devoid of Wallis blue, the papers rushed the news to their female readers. When the press reported that the

Windsors were planning a trip to the States, manufacturers hurried copies of her most recent hat purchases—medium-large black-felt models "in the halo-shaped, off-the-face design that the Duchess favors"—into production for the American consumer. Wallis's carefully created look had generated wide appeal.

In 1940, Wallis achieved the pinnacle of fashion success when the Paris designers named her the best-dressed woman in the world in a tie with her sister-in-law, the duchess of Kent. The judges praised Wallis as having the "smartest wardrobe any woman in the world has ever picked." Wallis would remain on the best-dressed list for forty years and was one of the four women first inducted into the International Best-Dressed List Hall of Fame when it was created in 1959.

In 1940, Prime Minister Winston Churchill appointed the Duke of Windsor to a five-year term as governor of the Bahamas. The duke and duchess tried to make the most of this small appointment, but could not help feeling isolated on the island of Nassau. During their stay in the Bahamas, Wallis

clothes, but after a lifetime of meticulous attention to her wardrobe it had become a way of life. She remained committed to the style of dress she had adopted during the 1930s, and rarely wavered from the formula, making sure that her skirts remained at the length she considered most flattering to her figure. By the 1950s, however, her ensembles no longer had the same captivating presence that they did when she wore cutting-edge haute couture in the 1930s. Shying away from avant-garde fashion, the day and evening apparel she chose became little more than a backdrop for her stunning collection of unusual jewels. Consumed with a need to maintain the standard of appearance she and the duke had set years earlier, Wallis insisted that all formal photographic portraits of them be touched up to remove wrinkles and other signs of aging.

During this period, she shopped at the couture houses of Balenciaga and Dior. When Dior's "New Look" emerged after the Second World War, Wallis briefly experimented with the new style, but the full-skirted creations with their cinched-in waists were unflattering on her small, angular frame. She instead turned to the designer's alternate collection, which featured a slim silhouette. She also refashioned jewelry that the duke had given her, since they no longer had the funds to purchase new gems on a regular basis. She delighted in large, colorful stones in settings that were reminiscent of costume jewelry, and was amused by the reactions of people who had presumed that the stones couldn't possibly be real.

By the 1960s, her position as one of the most fashionable women in the world was secure. The Spadea pattern company persuaded her to design a line of dress patterns under her name. The distraction thoroughly amused her:

convinced Mainbocher and the New York designer Hattie Carnegie to send seamstresses to the governor's house to fit her for lightweight day and evening clothes suitable for the tropical heat in Nassau. When the Windsors paid a visit to the United States in 1941, they were received by enthusiastic crowds larger than those that had turned out to greet King George VI and Queen Elizabeth on their state visit three years earlier. And while the attention the duke and duchess received in the States only served to annoy the royal family, it was a bit of vindication for the exiled Windsors.

After the war, the Windsors returned to France, purchasing a town house in the Bois de Boulogne (the same house Princess Diana was traveling to when she was tragically killed in Paris), and a country home outside of Paris, which they called The Mill. For the remainder of their married life they would divide their time among the two French homes, a suite in the Waldorf-Astoria Hotel in New York, and the homes of various friends in Palm Beach.

By the 1950s, Wallis no longer needed to validate her place in society through her

"I've done two or three hundred patterns so far, and I love doing them. I usually take my ideas from the clothes I wish I could wear—so as not to put every other woman in round high necks and the severe line I insist on for myself." Wallis was clever; why make it easy for other women to copy her distinctive look by providing patterns?

In 1967, the Duke and Duchess of Windsor were invited to London to attend the dedication of a memorial to the duke's late mother, Queen Mary. It was the first time Wallis had seen her in-laws since the years prior to her marriage thirty years earlier. Over the next several years, the duke began to suffer numerous health problems, including heart and eye trouble and cancer of the throat. During a state visit to Paris in 1972, Queen Elizabeth II, her husband, Prince Philip, and their son Charles, Prince of Wales, paid a visit to the dying duke at the Windsors' home in the Bois de Boulogne, where they were greeted by the duchess. On May 28, 1972, the duke died and, as he had requested, was buried in the royal cemetery at Frogmore near Windsor. The duchess accompanied her husband's coffin to England, where the queen invited her to stay at Buckingham Palace, a courtesy that Wallis did not expect. She brought with her a new black dress and coat that Givenchy had rushed to complete so that she would be appropriately dressed for the funeral. Consumed with her appearance even in bereavement, she brought her hairdresser, the French stylist Alexandre, with her to England.

Wallis survived the duke by fourteen years. In 1975, her health began to decline, and her final years were spent in the Paris town house, where she lived as a near-recluse, attended by her faithful servants and a few close friends. She died on April 2, 1986, and was buried beside the duke at Frogmore. To the surprise of many, her will ordered that all her jewels be sold for the benefit of the Institut Louis Pasteur in Paris. The auction would violate the duke's last wish: in one final romantic gesture, he had asked that all the gems in his wife's jewelry be removed from their settings so that no other woman would ever wear the jewels he had given her as a sign of his love. When the collection was auctioned in Geneva in 1987, the jewels, which were valued at seven million dollars, sold for fifty-one million; people were willing to part with a great deal of money in order to own a piece of the most remarkable romance of the twentieth century.

The mystique of the Duke and Duchess of Windsor was rekindled years later when the contents of the Windsors' Paris home was auctioned at Sotheby's in New York in early 1998. Enormous public interest drove prices skyward; even the most mundane artifacts were snatched up by collectors and dilettantes alike, perhaps with the knowledge that these keepsakes invoked a notion of romance and indeed were symbolic of an era that could never be recaptured.

This sketch by Cecil Beaton captures Wallis playing her favorite role—an international hostess of great skill.

Grace Kelly Grimaldi

Grace Kelly's rise to Hollywood stardom, her classic beauty, and fairy-tale marriage to a European prince enthralled American women during the second half of the twentieth century.

Hollywood in the 1950s produced two enduring female archetypes. One, the buxom bombshell, was embodied by countless full-figured stars and starlets—most notably Marilyn Monroe. The other was the beautiful, demure, and sophisticated socialite epitomized by Grace Kelly. While the first archetype is still with us, the second has found few imitators. In an era of bland suburbanization and mass production, Grace Kelly exuded high style, quality, and, in her own way, a subtle sensuality. Her life was a blueprint for the American dream: the grand-daughter of Irish immigrants, she became one of Hollywood's most popular stars. In a remarkably short career, she worked with some of the biggest names in show business, including Clark Gable, Gary Cooper, Bing Crosby, Cary Grant, Jimmy Stewart, William Holden, and Alfred Hitchcock. Then, at the pinnacle of her success in 1956, with her reputation firmly in place as one of America's leading actresses and biggest box-office draws, Grace Kelly turned her back on Hollywood to marry a European prince.

To American women, Grace Kelly was the ultimate symbol of the independent, successful woman, and her admirers emulated the fashions she popularized in her films as well as the similarly stylish clothes she was seen wearing in magazine and newspaper photographs. Pearl necklaces and gloves were her favorite accessories; her famous blonde hair was always smoothly coiffed in a flattering pageboy. The clean, classic lines of her onscreen and offscreen clothes were copied by women throughout the country. And while the look became synonymous with 1950s glamour, it was also a reflection of Grace's personal sense of style, which relied on fashions that were flattering to her figure and coloring. Until her death in 1982, she would continue to take a principled approach to clothes, understanding that poise and consistency were essential to her ever-polished public image.

Grace Patricia Kelly was born on November 12, 1929, the third child and middle daughter in a family of four children. Her father, John B. Kelly, was a first-generation Irish-American with a highly competitive nature and drive to succeed. He started out as a bricklayer and eventually became a successful contractor. Her mother, Margaret Katherine Majer, was the daughter of German immigrants. She, too, was ambitious, becoming the first woman to teach physical education at the University of Pennsylvania. When John Kelly and Margaret Majer married on January 30, 1924, she converted to her husband's Roman Catholic faith.

Grace grew up in the large colonial-style home her father had built for his family in the suburbs of Philadelphia. Although very wealthy, the Kellys were barred from elite Main Line society because John Kelly was a self-made man who had once worked with his hands. The family didn't seem to mind the social exclusion, preferring a credo of hard work and athletic achievement. Margaret Kelly was a strict matriarch who insisted that her daughters learn how to cook, clean, and sew. She also ran a frugal household and expected her children to be cost-conscious.

Grace Patricia Kelly, age twelve.

Grace and her sisters, Peggy and Lizanne, attended convent schools near their home. When she was eleven years old, Grace appeared in a performance by the Academy Players of Philadelphia, a local theater group. Thrilled by the experience, she developed a strong interest in acting. When she graduated from high school, she applied to Bennington College but was rejected because of her poor scores in mathematics. She then convinced her parents to let her apply to New York's American Academy of Dramatic Arts, whose graduates include Katharine Hepburn, Kirk Douglas, and Lauren Bacall; after an audition she was accepted into the program.

Concerned that her strikingly beautiful young daughter might be corrupted by living in New York, Margaret Kelly insisted that Grace live in the Barbizon Hotel, an establishment that provided rooms and strict supervision for single women. Grace thrived in New York, relishing her first taste of independence. For eight hours a day she attended classes at the Academy in the attic studios of Carnegie Hall. In her free time, Grace began modeling and was soon earning nearly four hundred dollars a week. With her blonde hair, riveting blue eyes, and exquisite features, she embodied the postwar vision of the all-American girl; she was soon featured on the covers of *Cosmopolitan* and *Redbook*, and in print and television ads for products ranging from Electrolux to Old Gold tobacco. Still photography, however, failed to capture Grace's essence; one photographer was heard to say that she was "what we call 'nice clean stuff' in our business. She's not a top model and never will be. She's the girl next door. No glamour, no oomph, no cheesecake." What the photographer failed to see was the fire beneath the icy exterior, something Alfred Hitchcock would draw out of Grace only a short while later.

While attending the Academy, Grace began developing her style of dress. The school prospectus outlined what it expected of its students in the way of dress and comportment: "The actor and actress should know how to dress with fitness, good taste and sincerity, as well as with a knowledge of harmony and contrast in color and of suitability to one's own figure and physical characteristics." Grace learned that clothes and makeup could transform a person's image, and she began to experiment

Grace preferred modest dresses, low-heeled shoes, hats with small veils, and, at all times, gloves.

the stage role of the daughter in the Strindberg tragedy *The Father,* costarring Raymond Massey. She made her Broadway debut in 1949 to favorable reviews, but after two months the show closed and Grace was again looking for work. Soon, however, she found success in the relatively new and talent-hungry medium of television, performing in more than sixty shows between 1950 and 1953. The steady income from her television work allowed Grace to move out of the Barbizon and into an apartment of her own on Sixty-second Street and Third Avenue.

with developing her own style. Wanting to be taken seriously as an actress, the image Grace projected in New York was composed and dignified. As she studied make-up at the Academy, she realized that her delicate features and coloring were not suited to the boldly colored lips, darkly drawn eyebrows, and thick coats of mascara that were popular in the late 1940s. Instead, she wore very little makeup and, through subtle coloring, emphasized her best features. The result was a fresh, natural look that seemed timeless and immune to fads; keeping to this style throughout her life, Grace never appeared either trendy or out of style.

When she completed her two-year course of study at the Academy, Grace's reserved style of dress failed to entice casting directors, who were accustomed to actresses who dressed in a more overtly sexual manner. As she made the rounds of auditions in New York, she met with repeated rejection; her cool, elegant demeanor was difficult for directors to categorize. She eventually landed

In 1950, she appeared in her first film, *Fourteen Hours.* Although her role was small, it gave her a taste of Hollywood and the art of filmmaking, and with her earnings she splurged and bought herself a mink stole. She was also beginning to generate interest among studio executives, who saw a promising property in the twenty-two-year-old newcomer. Eventually, she signed a seven-year contract with Metro-Goldwyn-Mayer, which offered a salary of $750 a week and a clause allowing one year off for every two years worked, so Grace could perform in the theater in New York—an unusual concession for a studio to make to an unknown actress at the time. That same year, in 1952, she was cast as Gary Cooper's young Quaker wife in the classic western *High Noon.* While in Hollywood filming

Alfred Hitchcock in that director's masterful thriller *Dial M for Murder*. Under Hitchcock's brilliant direction, a new dimension in Grace's acting emerged. While her cool reserve had previously made her appear distant, Hitchcock recognized in her a quality he called "sexual elegance"—the ability to cloak smoldering passion with an elegant veneer. During shooting, Hitchcock developed respect for Grace's intuitive skills, an unusual accolade from a director who once referred to actors as "cattle." In the key scene in the movie—in which Grace's character answers the telephone in the middle of the night, not realizing there is a killer hired by her husband lurking in the apartment—Hitchcock had intended for Grace to wear an elaborate velvet robe he had chosen because of the way the light played on its plush surface. Grace argued that if she heard the phone ring in the middle of the night, she wouldn't struggle into a robe first, but would answer it in her nightgown. Hitchcock agreed to shoot the scene her way, and was so pleased by the result that, as Grace remembered, "I had his confidence as far as wardrobe was concerned. He gave me a great deal of liberty in what I would wear in the next two pictures."

In her second pairing with Hitchcock, Grace co-starred with Jimmy Stewart in *Rear Window*, the story of a photojournalist who, confined to his apartment with a broken leg, believes he has witnessed one of his neighbors committing a murder. Playing Lisa Fremont, Stewart's society girlfriend, Grace wore a remarkable collection of "New Look"–inspired costumes designed by Edith Head. Grace shone as Lisa. She succeeded in bringing an emotional depth to her role as an alluring woman who subtly reveals her passionate nature. The role propelled Grace into the pantheon of Hollywood stars. She became the number one box-office draw in the country and remained in the top three until her retirement in 1956.

When the movie was released in 1954, movie marquees began dropping Jimmy Stewart and Alfred Hitchcock's names in favor of Grace's. Seemingly overnight, her face began to appear on magazine covers throughout the country, among them *Time, Look, The Saturday Evening*

the movie, Grace invited her sisters to stay with her at the elegant Chateau Marmont hotel, where they served as her chaperones on evenings out. Grace was wary of the Hollywood publicity machine and was not willing to sacrifice her acting reputation for the sake of self-promotion. She refused to pose in a bathing suit for studio publicity shots and rejected requests from the public relations department to provide her measurements for press releases. MGM, accustomed to publicity-hungry starlets, was at a loss as to how to promote this headstrong young actress.

When *High Noon* was released, Grace was disappointed in her acting, which she felt was wooden next to the expressiveness of Gary Cooper's Academy Award–winning performance. She returned to New York and enrolled in Sanford Meisner's Neighborhood Playhouse on Fifty-fourth Street in Manhattan, in the hope of increasing the emotional depth of her acting.

Nineteen fifty-three would prove to be Grace's most productive year in Hollywood. She appeared in six films, and, despite her self-doubt, *High Noon* turned out to be a big hit with moviegoers. She was soon cast in her next film, John Ford's *Mogambo*, which would be shot in Africa with Clark Gable and Ava Gardner. While the film received mixed reviews, Grace received kudos for her performance and, no less important, her ability to hold her own with Gable; she was nominated for an Academy Award for Best Supporting Actress.

Soon after, Grace appeared in her first starring role and embarked upon her first collaboration with

Post, McCall's, and *Ladies' Home Journal,* as journalists attempted to uncover the real woman behind the cool demeanor. Frank Scully described Grace's overnight success in *Variety:* "Never have I watched a girl climb upward with such undiminished power, unaided by scandal or any other agencies of the sort of notoriety that the modern world too frequently confuses with fame." In a similar vein, *The New York Times* noted, "Every so often a personality will rocket to the top of the motion picture world in a dazzling ascent to success. Some attain it by sheer physical allure and little else. In others, it can be traced to a remarkable affinity for publicity. And then there is Grace Kelly. That Miss Kelly is beautiful only a madman would deny. Very few performers can generate publicity as easily as Miss Kelly but it is not manufactured. And she can act, in a field where acting sometimes is only a secondary consideration. Some veteran chroniclers of the cinema contend her potent public appeal lies in the fact that she is a lady, insists on being treated like one, and the public, satiated with mere pulchritude, seems to like those qualitites." But perhaps *Time* magazine summed it up best in the title of its 1954 cover story on Grace, "Gentleman Prefer Ladies."

As her popularity soared, the Grace Kelly look quickly took hold among American women. The classic lines of her clothes, coupled with her stunning beauty, became the fashion ideal, replacing the buxom model Hollywood had promoted through actresses such as Marilyn Monroe and Jane Russell. Of course, for most women, it was much easier to copy Grace's understated clothes than to dress like a sex symbol. As Hollywood publicists began to promote Grace Kelly's patrician upbringing and solid family values, she became the prototype for the ideal American woman espoused by women's magazines in the 1950s. Her neat hair and makeup, figure-flattering shirtwaist dresses and tailored suits, low-heeled shoes, her discriminating use of jewelry—preferably pearls—and, of course, her gloves became a model for young suburban housewives in booming postwar America. Grace paid attention to

At left, Grace appears in her pivotal scene from Dial M for Murder. *Her appearance as a fashion editor in* Rear Window *(right) catapulted Grace into stardom. She frequently appeared on the covers of popular magazines.*

clothes but was not a clotheshorse; indeed, her upbringing made her rather thrifty. Her one weakness was gloves, which she purchased in great quantity and at great expense.

Like so many beautiful actresses who fear their looks might prevent them from being taken seriously, Grace yearned for movie roles that would emphasize her dramatic skill. When she learned that a pregnant Jennifer Jones had to drop out of *The Country Girl*, an upcoming film by to be directed by George Seaton, Grace leapt at the chance to play Georgie Elgin, the dowdy wife of a washed-up, alcoholic performer played by Bing Crosby. After consulting Edith Head, Grace went to her audition wearing no makeup and a dreary-looking housedress, her hair uncombed and unwashed. Realizing she had the talent for the role, the producers were convinced by her appearance that she could look the part as well. As part of her immersion in her role and in her effort to be taken seriously as an actress, Grace began to dress, as her

Grace Kelly's enormous popularity inspired McCall and other pattern companies to introduce designs like those shown above that resembled her wardrobe for Rear Window. *The actress wears the exquisite dress designed for the film by Edith Head in the photo at right.*

then-fiancé, Oleg Cassini, noted, "[like] a great beauty trying to pass as a maiden schoolteacher." Cassini, who had previously been married to actress Gene Tierney and had designed costumes for movies, knew a bit about creating a look for an actress. He encouraged Grace to dress more glamorously when she wasn't in character. He reportedly told her, "When you arrive at the studio each morning, don't come as Georgie Elgin. Be glamorous, be perfect—and then become your character. It will create a mystique about you. It will enhance your reputation. Show them you are more than just the role you are playing at this moment; show them you can be glamorous and sexy, too . . . You are becoming a major star, and should be a leader in fashion also." Grace took Cassini's advice to heart, recognizing her responsibility as a celebrity and a role model. Cassini helped her choose items from his own collections and designed a few pieces exclusively for her. His contribution to the Grace Kelly look was to put her in elegant, subdued dresses that set off her regal carriage, her remarkable complexion, and her golden hair. The result of this meticulously arranged wardrobe was, among other things, inclusion in the best-dressed list of 1955.

Grace Kelly was nominated for an Academy Award as Best Actress for her work in *The Country Girl*. At the awards ceremony on March 30, 1955, the star arrived wearing an evening gown, designed for her by Edith Head, of ice-blue silk with a fitted bodice, thin shoulder straps, and a tubular skirt that pulled back to form a sweeping train. Grace's fiercest competition for the Oscar came from Judy Garland, who was nominated for her performance in *A Star Is Born*. When William Holden, her costar in *The Country Girl*, announced her name as the winner, Grace wept openly. As she posed with her statuette alongside the Best Actor winner, Marlon Brando, her composure quickly returned; when photographers asked her to kiss Brando, she responded coolly, "I believe he should kiss me." As any man in his position would, Brando complied.

Later that year, Grace was invited to the Cannes Film Festival as a guest of the French government. Numerous photo opportunities had been scheduled during the trip.

When she arrived in Cannes, Grace discovered that there was no electricity in her hotel due to a workers' strike. Unable to iron her garments and expected in Monaco imminently, she settled for the one outfit that had survived the flight with a minimal amount of creasing: a long-sleeved black dress with a fitted bodice and full skirt that was patterned with large cabbage roses. As a testimony to Grace's popularity, this dress was reproduced by The McCall Pattern Company.

including one for the French magazine *Paris Match*. It was arranged that Grace, soon after arriving in France, would meet Prince Rainier of Monaco, who would lead her on a tour of his three-hundred-room palace as the photographers clicked away. Although the prince was late for their meeting, the guided tour went off without a hitch. It appeared that His Serene Highness was quite taken with the beautiful movie star.

Grace and Rainier didn't see each other again until Christmas, when the prince came to the United States and was invited by a mutual acquaintance to attend the Kelly family's annual Christmas Eve party. People at the party later acknowledged that there was definitely an attraction between Grace and the prince. Over the holidays, the two spent a great deal of time together, and soon there was little doubt that they had fallen in love. Both quickly expressed a desire to get married: the prince, then thirty-two, needed to provide an heir to the throne to prevent the principality from reverting to France; Grace, who strongly believed in traditional values, wanted a family and a husband who would not be overshadowed by her success and fame. They became engaged on New Year's Eve, and on January 5, 1956, a press conference was held in the Kelly home to announce the wedding. Wearing a gold brocade shirtdress, Grace sat next to the prince, looking helpless while journalists and photographers nearly crushed each other as they jockeyed for a clear shot of the newly engaged couple, wreaking havoc on the Kellys' home in the process. The press conference that day was but a foreshadowing of the media frenzy that would follow.

Grace returned to California to shoot what would become her last movie, *High Society*, a musical rendition of *The Philadelphia Story*. She wore her engagement ring on camera, a twelve-carat emerald-cut diamond. Rainier returned to Monaco, where the Monegasques were celebrating the fact that their prince was finally marrying. In the 1950s, Monaco was a little-recognized spot along the French Riviera that was principally known for its casino. Many Americans, in fact, wondered if the prince of this tiny country was a worthy husband for their box-office queen. Hollywood in particular was baffled: how could Grace Kelly consider leaving such a flourishing film career?

As excitement over the April nuptials increased, the Kelly family, shrewdly anticipating potential commercial exploitation, took out an advertisement in *Women's Wear Daily*, threatening legal action if any manufacturers tried to capitalize on Grace Kelly's wedding to Prince Rainier. They intended to prevent any company from using without permission the royal couple's names or seals to promote products. The wedding of the Hollywood movie star and the European prince was becoming the biggest media spectacle since the coronation of Queen Elizabeth II in 1953.

After the filming of *High Society* wrapped in early March, Grace spent the weeks prior to her departure for Monaco putting together her trousseau. Always thoroughly prepared for every part she played, she concentrated with equal intensity on her forthcoming role as princess of Monaco. To assemble her wardrobe, she consulted with Eleanor Lambert, the fashion arbiter who had resurrected the best-dressed list after its demise during World War II. The trousseau consisted of six cocktail dresses, four summer dresses, two evening dresses, two ball gowns, several light coats, a dozen hats, shoes (all with low heels so she wouldn't tower over the prince), and her nine costumes from *High Society*, which were a gift from MGM. The most expensive items were three

Both wearing dark glasses, the actress and her fiancé arrive at the home of Grace's parents for a press conference to announce their engagment.

furs she purchased before the wedding: a full-length Canadian sable coat, a full-length leopard-skin coat, and a mink jacket. In all, her trousseau cost about twenty-five thousand dollars, a large amount for the day, but not extraordinary next to the colossal sums regularly spent by the social elite.

Grace left for Monaco on April 4, 1956, along with seventy members of the Kelly family. She was met at the pier in New York by hordes of photographers and celebrity-watchers. On board the *Constitution*, Grace held a press conference in the observation lounge. As the nearly two hundred reporters and photographers pushed and strained against each other, a riot nearly broke out. Grace remained calm and composed, giving brief responses to the many shouted questions that managed to reach her. The ship's whistle put an end to the press conference, but even at sea there was

no escaping the media; several leading newspapers had booked passage for their reporters. Despite the discomfort their presence must have caused, Grace was polite and courteous to the reporters at all times.

On the morning of April 12, the *Constitution* sailed into Monaco's harbor and was met by Prince Rainier's yacht, the *Deo Juvante II*. Grace crossed the gangplank wearing a navy-blue silk dress with a matching coat, a white corsage, white gloves, pearl necklace, and a large white hat, which, to the disappointment of press and public alike, hid her face. The *Deo Juvante II* made its way to shore, where crowds broke into cheers as cannons and ship sirens sounded a welcome. Above it all, a plane owned by Aristotle Onassis dropped red and white carnations—the colors of Monaco. David Schoenbrun of CBS's Paris news bureau noted that there was more noise when Grace Kelly arrived in Monaco than on D-Day.

Over the next week, more than fifteen hundred reporters from Europe and America arrived to cover the April 19 wedding, which was soon to be one of the first great live televised events, with the proceedings set to be broadcast throughout Europe to more than thirty million people in nine countries. For their chance to see the wedding, Americans would have to wait until the newsreels arrived.

As required by the Napoleonic Code, which was observed in Monaco, Grace Kelly and Prince Rainier were married in both civil and religious ceremonies. The civil wedding took place on April 18 in the throne room of the palace in front of one hundred witnesses, including family members, dignitaries, and heads of state. Both wedding dresses

Grace never lost her poise in the crush of photographers aboard the Constitution *before it set sail, bringing her to Monaco for her wedding.*

were gifts to the bride from MGM and had been designed by the studio's chief costume designer, Helen Rose, who had dressed Grace for her roles in *High Society* and *The Swan*. The dress for the civil ceremony was a semiformal suit of beige alençon lace over pale, rose-colored silk taffeta. The lace was delicately sewn to the silk to create a brocaded, three-dimensional effect. The jacket had three-quarter-length sleeves, a high neck with lace-covered buttons down the front, and a full skirt that ended at mid-calf, all accompanied by matching shoes and kid gloves.

That evening, Grace and the prince attended a gala performance of a ballet commissioned in honor of the new princess of Monaco. Grace's appearance that night was majestic; she wore a satin-and-organza dress by Lanvin that was encrusted with pearls, rhinestones, and opaque sequins. She also wore a diamond tiara and a $100,000 diamond necklace that was a wedding gift from the people of Monaco.

The next morning, Grace was escorted by her father, John Kelly, into the Cathedral of Saint Nicholas, where she was married to Prince Rainier in front of six hundred guests and one hundred lucky reporters. The wedding gown, which its designer described as the most costly she had ever created, was made of exquisite fabrics in a stylish and flattering silhouette. The gown consisted of a bodice of antique lace, long sleeves with scallops at the wrist, a standing collar with buttons down the front, a silk cummerbund, and a bell-shaped skirt of silk taffeta with a ten-foot train of silk and lace. Covering her chignon was a close-fitting headdress with a lace veil embroidered with thousands of tiny pearls. In place of a bouquet, Grace carried a silk-covered missal with a small cluster of lilies of the valley. The bridesmaids wore gowns of yellow silk organza with matching hats that had been designed by Helen Rose and made by Neiman Marcus.

While appearing more relaxed than she did at the civil ceremony, Grace's chief recollection of her wedding day was the cameras and microphones hidden in the flower arrangements on the altar and hanging from the rafters of the church. After a luncheon at the palace for the wedding guests, Grace and Rainier departed for their honeymoon aboard the royal yacht, where they were able to recover some of the privacy they had lost during their engagement.

In August, the palace announced that Princess Grace was pregnant and expecting the couple's first child in February.

After the wedding, Grace donated her gown to the Philadelphia Museum of Art, where it remains one of their most popular artifacts. The museum receives many requests for photos from prospective brides who wish to copy the gown.

American women were enthralled by the elegance of Grace Kelly's wedding (above). One bride in Louisville, Kentucky (below), appears to invoke the magic of the royal nuptials at her own 1956 ceremony. Like Grace, she stands apart from her bridesmaids.

After the wedding and her retirement from acting, Princess Grace hoped that the public's interest in her would diminish. Her hopes were in vain. Americans craved stories and pictures of the Hollywood movie star turned princess; tourism in Monaco also increased dramatically. The former movie star's presence lent an air of dignity and refinement to the Riviera principality. Princess Grace and Prince Rainier, rulers of one of the tiniest countries in Europe, were invited on official and semiofficial trips to the United States, France, England, Spain, Ireland, and the Vatican. Grace's arrival in the States, shortly after her first pregnancy had been announced, mesmerized the country and drew more attention from the press and public than the recent visits of the presidents of Italy and Mexico.

In an effort to control the amount and accuracy of information about them in the press, Princess Grace and Prince Rainier hired a publicist and decided to commission one or two exclusive articles a year from respected publications. Princess Grace, having survived Hollywood's publicity machine, was determined to control the media's access to her family. She wisely bargained for the right to approve all copy and photographs whenever she granted an interview. Foreshadowing what would happen to the Kennedys during their years in the White House, the public began to take for granted their right to know about the lives of the royal family in Monaco. This sense of public entitlement, in turn, was seen by the press as a mandate to adopt increasingly intrusive strategies to report on the life of the royal couple—and ultimately of anyone in the public eye.

Princess Grace took her new responsibilities seriously. First and foremost, she was a wife and mother. Being a traditional woman who put the welfare of her family first, she lavished love and attention on her three children, Caroline, Albert, and Stephanie. She took her role as princess equally seriously and saw it as her duty to look after the people of Monaco and provide social and cultural initiatives for them. She was president of the Monaco Red Cross, she instituted the Princess Grace Foundation to support young people in the arts, and she also established a garden club that encouraged the study of botany. In addition, she became active in the World Wildlife Fund, a cause that ultimately led her to stop wearing fur. And, in 1976, Princess Grace made a return to the stage to do poetry readings for charitable events, thrilled to resurrect the skills that she had laid aside twenty years before.

On average days, Grace Kelly appeared to retain the classic look she had developed as an actress, wearing the comfortable clothes she preferred. But by night she fulfilled her image as a royal dignitary. For public occasions, she preferred to wear light colors, dressing in apricots, pale yellows, blues, and bright pinks. Her favorite designers, Marc Bohan of Dior and Vera Maxwell, became personal friends and were devoted to the princess throughout her life, as were many of the people she worked with after she arrived in Monaco. Grace tended to become very attached to her clothes, particularly if she found an ensemble unusually flattering or comfortable; indeed, her husband and her designers had to encourage her to make new purchases from time to time.

One of the people Princess Grace grew close to soon after her marriage was the famous French hairstylist Alexandre, whose clients included the Duchess of Windsor and Elizabeth Taylor. Although Grace was accustomed to doing her own hair, she found that the climate in Monaco made her fine, blonde hair difficult to manage. With Alexandre's encouragement, she kept her hair at shoulder length, and for evening she would attach one of six hairpieces he created for her. Each hairpiece was kept in its own numbered box, with a corresponding illustration by the stylist to remind her how to attach it to her hair. By all accounts, Grace found this to be a simple and elegant solution, especially when traveling.

In 1956, conscious of the fact that her pregnancy was already apparent, Princess Grace began to carry a large, square Hermès handbag that she had purchased in Paris; she would conveniently hold it in front of her whenever the paparazzi were nearby. The handbag became popularly known as the Kelly bag.

On September 14, 1982, the news that Princess Grace had died in an automobile accident along the curving roads above Monaco shocked the world. Grace Kelly was only fifty-two at the time of her death, making the tragedy even sharper. In the more than twenty-seven years that had passed since her success in *Rear Window*, Americans had developed a deep and abiding love for Princess Grace. The details of her royal lifestyle and her successes and setbacks as a wife and mother filled America's media. Many woke up early on Saturday, September 18, to watch her funeral at the same cathedral where she had been married; they saw dignitaries from around the world pay their respects, among them Diana, Princess of Wales, First Lady Nancy Reagan, members of the royal houses of Spain, Sweden, and the Netherlands, and her old Hollywood friends Frank Sinatra and Cary Grant.

Many years after her death, the brilliant aura of Princess Grace continues to glimmer on the American cultural and aesthetic landscape. She remains the classic embodiment of the chic, stylish fashions of the 1950s and 1960s, which are still copied by contemporary designers. Even today, Americans tend to identify the 1950s look with the fashion elements Grace wore so well—shimmering fabrics, coatdresses, and cool clear colors. Driving the lasting appeal of Grace's style is, no doubt, her equally enduring spirit. Edith Head put it simply: "She never dressed to attract attention; she never dressed like an actress; she dressed like Grace Kelly . . ."

> *"The basis for her success is her combination of freshness, ladylike virtue and underlying sex appeal."*
> —Life *magazine, 1954*

Women of the Stage &

of the
Screen

Fashion has always been about role-playing—about crafting an identity through clothes, appearance, and image. It is no wonder, then, that the American pursuit of fashion shares its deepest roots with the history of stage and screen—and, more specifically, with the extraordinary personalities that have captivated American audiences. America's fascination with actresses and performers is almost as old as the American stage itself. In the 1830s, Fanny Kemble's riveting interpretations of Shakespeare's classic heroines inspired scores of female fans. Some were content to copy her hairstyle and bonnets, while others, such as the great American actress Charlotte Cushman, were inspired to embark on their own careers in the theater. A half-century later, a young Ethel Barrymore fascinated a new generation of female fans, eliciting the same strong bond with her audience that Fanny Kemble had enjoyed before her.

When Hollywood emerged as the country's entertainment capital in the early twentieth century, a new type of icon was born—the movie star. Almost from its inception, the movie industry set out to entice female fans with lavish sets, handsome leading men, and beautiful women dressed in gorgeous costumes. The unprecedented reach of the Hollywood movie machine revolutionized the way fashion was marketed to middle-class women. Since it could take years for a movie to complete its run in theaters throughout the country, costume designers had to create screen wardrobes that would not easily become dated. Mail-order catalogues, department stores, and dress-pattern manufacturers were quick to link their fashion merchandise to successful Hollywood films. Middle-class women across the country were thus encouraged to buy a bit of screen magic.

One dress fad followed another as Hollywood paraded regiments of new starlets, and new styles, before a rapt public. In the early years of silent films, Mary Pickford's golden ringlets and girl-next-door looks became the American ideal. Then came the It Girl, Clara Bow, whose Cupid's-bow lips and penciled eyebrows helped introduce cosmetics into women's daily lives. Soon, Max Factor, a Polish immigrant, revolutionized makeup for the screen, helping to create the look of many of Hollywood's top female stars. Factor was responsible for tweezing Jean

Harlow's eyebrows into a thin line and dyeing her hair platinum blonde, inaugurating a hot new trend. The Hollywood-driven cosmetics craze led *Vogue* to comment in 1937, "The way you make up your lips, apply your rouge . . . ten to one it came from Hollywood and was devised either by or for some famous star."

Inevitably, the conservative American establishment was often at pains to keep up with Hollywood's frenetic trends. During World War II, when American women began copying Veronica Lake's hairstyle—which concealed one eye under a long, sultry wave—the United States Manpower Commission requested that Miss Lake alter her hairdo. The government commission was afraid that women factory workers would get their hair caught in the machinery. In the end, Veronica Lake toed the line, announcing in a government newsreel, "Any girl who wears her hair over one eye is silly. I certainly don't, except in pictures." The newsreel then cut to footage showing the film star's new, upswept hairdo.

Totally new or cleverly retro, the costumes meticulously created for the American cinema have never ceased to exert an enormous influence over what women wear. Whether it's Elizabeth Taylor's bouffant ball gown in *A Place in the Sun*, Faye Dunaway's stylish 1930s sweaters and berets from *Bonnie and Clyde*, or Diane Keaton's trendsetting thrift-shop wardrobe from *Annie Hall*, the clothes adorning the right star at the right time will inevitably make their way, in one form or another, into the closets of adoring fans.

Ethel Barrymore

Katharine Hepburn once said of Ethel Barrymore, "She has more friends than anyone I know, but she's not a dear soul. Barrymores don't come like that. She has a trenchant wit . . . She makes appallingly accurate observations." Indeed, the woman who preceded Helen Hayes as the first lady of American theater was well-schooled in the polite conventions lingering after the Victorian era, although years of self-sufficiency had made her a disinterested observer of human frailties and foibles. Ethel Barrymore's remarkable combination of femininity and independence became a touchstone for the generation of American women who came of age in the first two decades of the twentieth century. Ethel was part of the then-burgeoning "leisure class"—a unique constituency of mostly unmarried, educated urban women who were enjoying the sometimes frivolous amusements at their disposal. It was among such young, impressionable theatergoers that the matinee idols of the day found their following, and that Ethel Barrymore made her name as a stage icon, a fashion plate, and as the prototype of the "ideal American girl."

*E*thel Barrymore's mesmerizing stage presence, exquisite features, and stylish gowns made her one of the most emulated women of the early twentieth century. The actress and her brothers left a lasting imprint on the American theater. Above, she and John appear in A Slice of Life.

While some actors from theatrical families tell tales of being born in a trunk, or between acts, the Barrymores would never have allowed such a lowbrow entrance. Even before the turn of the century, this family seemed conscious of their reputation as one of America's acting dynasties—and of all the formalities the notion of dynasty entails. Ethel was born

Forced by financial circumstances to work, Ethel first appeared on stage when she was fourteen. For the next several years, she earned a meager living playing bit parts in touring theatrical companies. The photograph at right shows her in the 1896 production of Rosemary.

in Philadelphia on August 15, 1879. Her father, Maurice Barrymore, was a matinee idol and her mother, Georgiana "Georgie" Drew Barrymore, was a beloved comedienne. Ethel saw little of her parents as she grew up, since they were often touring in various productions. She and her older brother, Lionel, and younger brother, John, were raised by their maternal grandmother, Louisa Drew, also an actress and the first woman to manage a theater in the United States. The profits of that institution, the Arch Street Theater, in addition to the earnings of the many actors in the family, assured that the Barrymore children had a proper upbringing. Louisa Drew, or Mum Mum, as she was called by her grandchildren, considered the real-life social graces to be as important as memorizing one's lines for a role on stage. She insisted that the children speak with perfect diction, be punctual at all meals, and pay close attention to their grooming habits. As trying as these demands may have been for young Ethel—a tomboy at heart—they would pay off later, when her impeccable social skills won friends and admirers among the elite patrons of both English and American theater.

In 1883, Ethel and Lionel accompanied their parents on tour with one of the most famous actresses of the day, Madame Helena Modjeska. Georgie Barrymore and Madame Modjeska became close friends during the trip—so close that Georgie decided that her family would convert to the Modjeskas' Roman Catholic faith. As a result, when the tour was over, the Barrymore children were enrolled in Catholic boarding schools. Ethel was sent to a convent school, the Academy of Notre Dame in Philadelphia, where she felt quite at home studying piano, singing, and dancing. A talented pianist, she was encouraged in her pursuit by the sisters, and dreamed of one day studying abroad.

When Ethel was thirteen, Georgie Barrymore became quite ill. Because all the adults of the family were contractually committed to long-running plays, Ethel was taken out of school to accompany her mother to California, where, doctors hoped, the warm climate would restore Georgie's health. Having been quite literally cloistered at school, Ethel didn't fully comprehend what was happening, and grew even more confused when she witnessed her mother bid Maurice Barrymore a tearful good-bye. It was only on their arrival in Santa Barbara that Ethel understood that her mother was dying of tuberculosis. When Georgie succumbed, a short time later, it was left to Ethel to notify the rest of the family. She packed up her own and her mother's belongings and ordered a suitable black mourning dress—her first grown-up attire.

Ethel returned to the convent school, where she remained so cut off from the rest of her family that only after coming across a newspaper clipping, three months after her mother's death, did Ethel learn of her father's remarriage. She was devastated, deeming Maurice's actions unforgivable. It would be several years before she would attempt a full reconciliation with her father.

Not long afterward, the Barrymore finances began to crumble. Louisa Drew lost the Arch Street Theater and was forced to sell the family home. Just fourteen, Ethel was taken out of school to help support the family by joining the only profession any of them knew—acting. Leaving behind her dream of becoming a concert pianist, Ethel traveled to Montreal to join her grandmother and uncle, thus becoming the third generation of her family to take to the stage.

Estranged from her immediate family, Ethel was called upon to embark on a career for which she had no practical training. To make matters worse, Louisa Drew, then more than seventy years old, left the production and moved to New York, sending her granddaughter alone on tour with the company. Ethel made her debut in 1894 in a Canadian production of *The Rivals*, playing the small role of Julia. No one in the family had considered that she might not know how to act; Ethel was, after all, a Drew and a Barrymore. For the next several years, the young girl picked up acting jobs wherever she could. Her uncle John Drew, one of the most popular and talented actors of his day, introduced her to the noted theatrical producer Charles Frohman, who agreed to add Ethel to his roster. As they toured the country, Ethel couldn't ignore the irony of her life: as a bit player in the theater she made a meager living and was forced to find lodgings in the cheapest boarding houses and hotels; as the daughter

of two popular actors and the niece of John Drew, the doors of high society opened to her at every turn. Nearly every evening she had invitations to dances, concerts, and dinners. Her worst dilemma was trying to stretch her meager wardrobe into one suitable for the social whirl.

While on tour, Ethel received a telegram from Frohman offering her a small part in a London production starring William Gillette, the Connecticut-born actor who had won acclaim for his stage portrayal of Sherlock Holmes. She soon became a great success on the London stage, and, as in America, was courted by the best of society.

Ethel's time in London coincided with a transitional period in fashion; the hourglass silhouette of the Gay Nineties, characterized by large, leg-of-mutton sleeves and wide, stiff skirts, gave way to a slimmer silhouette. While the front of the bodice became fuller, sleeves were

As a young woman, Ethel displayed her grandmother's grace and poise—qualities that would later serve her both on and off the stage.

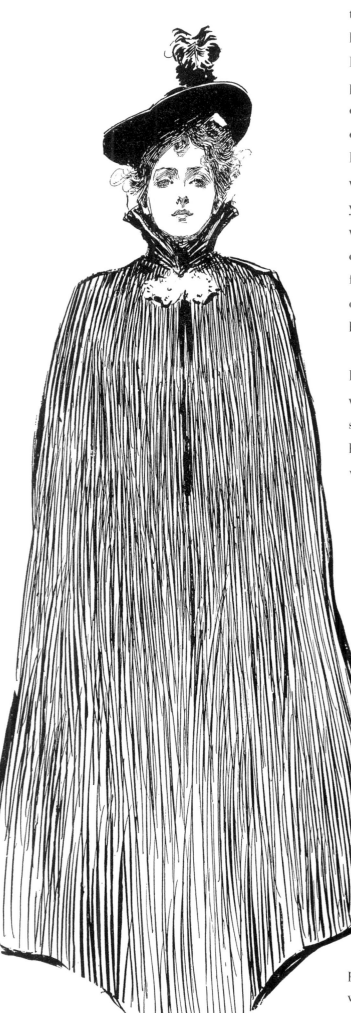

tapered, retaining just a little volume in the shoulder cap; the skirt, which lengthened at the back into a small train, lost some of its stiffness to fit more closely to the hips. In this changing fashion climate, eighteen-year-old Ethel finally came up with a solution to her wardrobe problem. "I had two dresses," she recalled in her memoirs, "one black and one white, which I found were quite enough for the highest and most exalted society. In London, somehow, people don't care who you are or what you have on; if they make up their minds they like you, they take you in and there you stay for all time." She was introduced to members of the royal family, was courted by the sons of England's aristocracy (including future prime minister Winston Churchill), and was the only actress invited to attend the garden party in celebration of Queen Victoria's Diamond Jubilee.

While Ethel was enjoying success abroad, Louisa Drew died in her sleep in New York. Ethel, as strong-willed as all the Drew women, effectively installed herself as the matriarch of her far-flung family, overseeing her two high-strung brothers. As her brother Lionel would recall in his autobiography, "Ethel was the only member of the family who managed in any way to look after any other member . . . Ethel, bless her, was always on hand when the chips were down."

Newspapers throughout Britain and the United States considered Ethel's life in England's social circles good copy. While some of the exploits they reported were exaggerated or even fabricated, they did a great deal to build an alluring image for the emerging young star. Good publicity notwithstanding, Ethel was concerned that her celebrated social life would overshadow her work as an actress, which she had embraced whole-heartedly. Although her American and English managers made no attempt to halt the publicity, Ethel disliked the constant stream of articles and photographs that appeared in newspapers and magazines. Looking back on this period, she once said, "The goldfish bowl has been one of the hardest things I have had to cope with. Nowadays, there are paid publicists; I would gladly have paid not to be written about." The zeal of reporters covering Ethel Barrymore occasionally reached absurd proportions:

when a ship sank near a yacht on which she was cruising, one newspaper overlooked the tragedy to report, "Ethel Barrymore Sees Vessel Sink."

Upon her return to the States in February of 1901, Ethel Barrymore appeared on Broadway in her first starring role, as Madame Trentoni in *Captain Jinks of the Horse Marines*, the story of an opera singer who comes to America seeking fame and fortune and finds love. The play was a smash hit, and Ethel was an overnight sensation. One evening, a month after the play's opening, Ethel glanced up at the marquee; there, for the first time, was her name in lights.

Within two years of her first Broadway success, Ethel was earning enough to rent her own apartment in New York, leaving behind the boardinghouses that she had lived in since her mother's death. Ethel's new home often served as a haven for her brothers, and she soon began to help them along in their own acting careers, encouraging Frohman to cast them whenever a suitable role appeared. As one of Frohman's leading actresses, Ethel found that she had substantial influence over her manager's decisions.

Ethel was by then fully recognized as the heir to a beloved theatrical dynasty, and the media rarely failed to remind its female readership of this fact. The press also recognized in her the ideals of young womanhood epitomized by the ubiquitous Gibson Girl. Although Ethel

Ethel became an overnight sensation after starring in Captain Jinks of the Horse Marines *(above). American audiences adored the independent spirit and captivating talent of the young actress, pictured here in the background photo.*

was acquainted with illustrator Charles Dana Gibson, she never posed for him. As a member of Gibson's social set, however, Ethel doubtless informed the artist's vision of the ideal woman. Soon a number of newspapers and periodicals had labeled Ethel the "ideal American girl." Her convent-school education, distinguished family, and the social acceptance she enjoyed among both British and American aristocracy made her, in the eyes of the press, the perfect role model for women coming of age in a new century. "There has been no better illustration of the power of personality on the stage than is furnished by Miss Ethel Barrymore," wrote *Ladies' Popular Monthly* in May of 1903. "Her rise to fame has been almost meteoric. To her credit it must be said that the public has grown to like her, for the simple reason that it considers her a splendid example of the finest type of American girl."

As tall and as thin as a Gibson Girl, Ethel had straight brown hair, topaz-colored eyes, the famous Barrymore chiseled profile, natural grace, and a deep, wonderful speaking voice that, in the days before amplification, reached every member of the theater audience. She had a genuine dislike for anything frilly and overdone, preferring simple and refined clothes. She didn't curl or tease her hair, as many young women did, but rather wore it in a modest pompadour with a low bun at the neck. Even as her career and her income soared, she maintained a simple approach to dress, shunning the ever-popular high necks and dog-collar necklaces in favor of well-cut, one-piece gowns with rounded necklines and little or no embellishment. Ethel once told a reporter that she preferred clothes she could wear all day and that would be suitable for any occasion. It was quite enough, she reckoned, to make several costume changes in a performance without having to endure this inconvenience in her private life.

Given her pragmatic attitude toward dress, Ethel was surprised to see that her choice of apparel had great impact. In 1908, an article appeared in *Ladies' Home Journal* under the title, "How Ethel Barrymore Thinks a Young Girl Should Dress." In it the author compared Ethel's influence on young women to the popularity of former First Lady Frances Folsom Cleveland twenty years earlier. "Miss Barrymore," the article read, "is the ideal American girl in looks. She has the height that our American artists have loved and popularized; she has the unaffected, wholesome ways of the outdoor girl . . . She has the clear, frank eyes, the straight, simply-arranged hair, the fresh, healthy color, the straightforward speech that our most-admired modern heroines have had. She is, in a word, the kind of girl nearly every other girl would dearly love to be, and so it is no wonder that her devotees have tried to copy her hairdressing, her walk, her gowns."

Issued Monthly
$3.00 a Year.

AUGUST 1906

Vol. VI. NO. 66.
25 c. a Copy.

THE THEATRE
ILLUSTRATED MAGAZINE
OF DRAMATIC AND MUSICAL ART.

The Theatre Magazine Co.,
26 W. 33d Street, New York.

ETHEL BARRYMORE

The graceful, turn-of-the-century silhouette was often heavily embellished, particularly on the bodice, with an extraordinary profusion of laces and ribbons. Ethel embraced a less elaborate style of dress that, in effect, emphasized the attributes of the wearer rather than the skills of her dressmaker or the size of her pocketbook. She once described her tastes to a reporter from *Ladies' Home Journal*: "I just hate conspicuousness in dress . . . I know lots of girls who would look perfectly charming if their dresses were more simply made. But they put a lot of fussy things on them, and they spoil their dresses and their own looks." The simple sophistication that Ethel Barrymore preferred was to become more prevalent in the years preceding World War I.

It is not surprising that around this time Ethel made the acquaintance of a notable peer—Alice Roosevelt—who shared Ethel's reputation as a prototypical Gibson Girl, a similarity the media promoted whenever the two appeared together in public. The young women soon became good friends. Once, while performing in Washington, Ethel was invited on an afternoon outing with Alice, Congressman Nicholas Longworth, and Marguerite Cassini, the daughter of the Russian ambassador. While Ethel accompanied Alice upstairs to the family quarters to fetch their hats, Nick and Marguerite remained downstairs in the White House receiving rooms. As the two women ascended in the elevator, Alice's brothers played a trick on her by stopping the lift between floors, trapping Alice and Ethel for an hour. Ethel remembered how furious Alice became as their cries for help went unheeded. Alice was sure that the ravishing Marguerite was making a move on her would-be suitor. Building on such shared experience, their friendship endured; in later years, whenever Ethel was in Washington performing, she would visit Alice and sometimes accompany her to the Senate gallery to listen to the debates.

A *few weeks after giving birth to her first child, Ethel returned to the stage to begin rehearsals for* Mid-Channel.

A*fter numerous well-publicized romantic exploits, in 1909 Ethel married Russell Colt, the grandnephew of Samuel Colt, inventor of the six-shooter revolver. Russell's wandering eye and reluctance to work for a living made the marriage rocky from the start. Over the next fourteen years they had three children, and following each birth Ethel returned to the stage after only a few weeks of recuperation in order to cover expenses. After the birth of her first son, Samuel, she debuted in her first dramatic lead on Broadway, in *Mid-Channel*, the story of a wealthy woman in an unhappy marriage. With rumors circulating that her own marriage was in jeopardy, many wondered how true to life Ethel's moving performance was. In 1923, she finally filed for divorce when Colt began conducting a bold affair with a married younger woman; Ethel never remarried.

In 1913, in an effort to support her family, Ethel found a part in a one-act play on the lucrative vaudeville circuit. She hired a cast, ran the rehearsals, and took *The Twelve Pound Look* on tour, playing to packed houses around the country. The play told the story of a woman in a dead-end marriage who preferred to divorce her husband and earn twelve pounds a week as a secretary rather than be supported by a man she despised. A good measure of the play's success was due to the fact that it echoed some of the most fundamental changes being made in society: women were gaining financial independence, and talk of female suffrage was growing louder and harder to ignore.

As middle-class women joined the workforce during the First World War, and became more socially active through women's clubs, their mode of dress adapted to these changes. The S-bend silhouette gave way to a leaner, more vertical line, with a slightly raised waistline, and straight skirts with hemlines that exposed the ankle; Ethel adopted this practical new silhouette, which suited her forward-thinking independence. The actress seemed to be calling for, and effecting, social change on several fronts—

in her bold dramatic productions, in her populist mode of dress, and in her remarkably independent lifestyle.

In the early 1890s, inventors such as Thomas Edison and the Lumière brothers perfected the technology of motion-picture production. Movie studios, which had been scattered along the East Coast and across the Midwest, began to relocate to California. This move had a double motive: California provided both abundant sunshine and a healthy distance from the Motion Picture Patents Company, an eastern trust that was attempting to force independent producers out of business. By 1913, Hollywood became America's filmmaking capital; by World War I, it dominated the industry internationally.

The burgeoning film industry sent flocks of movie producers out to scour the American theater for talent. Lionel Barrymore was the first in the family to try his hand, and to succeed, at movie acting. After witnessing her brother's success and noting the large salaries movie actors commanded, Ethel decided to work in the industry. The great theater actress brought Hollywood some much-needed dignity, and after she appeared in her first film, one critic wrote, "Girls, we're sure moving pictures are all right now, aren't we? Nothing lowbrow about them if Miss Barrymore loves them, is there? Our taste is vindicated!"

However, it was from Broadway that Ethel Barrymore received her most cherished honor: in 1928, the Shubert brothers gave her name to their newest theater. Despite this acclaim, the middle-aged Ethel found fewer and fewer roles coming her way. Finally, in 1940, she was offered a role that suited her age and talents, and as the English schoolteacher in *The Corn Is Green* Ethel Barrymore had her first big Broadway success in years. Four years later, she permanently staked her claim in the world of film when she won an Academy Award for

Later in her career, Ethel divided her time between roles on the New York stage and in Hollywood films. She is shown above in the 1940 Broadway hit The Corn Is Green. *The actress eventually moved to California, where she and her brothers, Lionel and John, often spent time together (left).*

Best Supporting Actress in *None But the Lonely Heart*, starring Cary Grant. Over the next five years she would act in sixteen feature films. Never afraid to tackle a new venue, Ethel Barrymore also performed in a number of radio and early television programs. In 1949, on her seventieth birthday, Ethel's remarkable career was celebrated with a radio program featuring fifty celebrities paying tribute to the undisputed "queen of the theater's royal family."

Ethel eventually settled in California. There, she endeared herself to a generation of Hollywood's elite, among them Katharine Hepburn, who admired her wit and found in her a kindred spirit. Ethel Barrymore died in her sleep on June 18, 1959, having lived long enough to survive both of her brothers and to witness a new generation of Barrymores embrace the family profession.

Ethel Barrymore became a Broadway star in part because she was young, attractive, and talented, and in part because of her family name. But her fame also had a deeper source, one that manifested itself both in her steadfast commitment to simplicity and in her choice to lead an independent life. She proved that the emancipated female could be strong-willed, self-assured, skilled in her chosen profession, and capable of managing her own affairs without the advice or consent of a husband—and still be feminine. During an era in which Americans were engaged in serious dialogue about the changing role of women, Ethel Barrymore stood as living proof that the successful, independent woman was part of the natural progression of the American spirit.

Revered for her talent and beauty, Ethel Barrymore left an indelible mark on the American stage and screen. The American artist James Montgomery Flagg immortalized her in the portrait shown at right.

became the accepted model that virtually all screen actresses, from the 1920s through the 1950s, would aspire to.

Gloria Swanson was born on March 27, 1898, in Chicago, Illinois. Her father, Joseph, was attached to the United States Army Transport unit, and Gloria and her mother, Addie, followed him to bases in Key West, Florida, and Puerto Rico. Trapped in an unhappy marriage, Addie Swanson threw all her love and energy into her only child. Although blessed with an olive complexion and riveting blue eyes, Gloria was not conventionally pretty: she had a long nose and large ears—features her mother found troubling.

Addie Swanson taught her young daughter how to dress in a flattering manner and how to develop her own independent style. Mrs. Swanson wanted Gloria to stand out, and as a result her daughter never dressed like other girls. Addie made many of Gloria's clothes herself and took pains to choose unusual coats, hats, and accessories that she thought would suit her daughter. Addie's efforts proved successful; Gloria became the girl all her classmates copied. She loved the beautiful clothes her mother made and seemed to have few apprehensions about being different from her friends. As Gloria entered her teenage years, she grew eager to wear the stylish long dresses and more mature ensembles of adult women.

By the time she was fifteen years old, Gloria Swanson was a clotheshorse. She appreciated well-made pieces that flattered her petite figure, and typically selected styles that would elongate her five-foot-one-inch frame. In 1913, after she and her mother had returned to

In her autobiography, Gloria recalled how her mother made her wear large ribbons and bows in her hair to camouflage her large ears.

Chicago, an aunt invited Gloria to accompany her on a tour of the Chicago-based Essanay Studios, where Charlie Chaplin had made some of his classic silent films. For her visit, Gloria chose an outfit her mother had recently made based on an ensemble worn by the famous ballroom dancer Irene Castle. Dressed in a black-and-white checked skirt, a black cutaway coat, and a green waistcoat with a "perky felt hat," Gloria toured the sets and watched the actors perform what, from her vantage point, seemed little more than a pantomime—which was indeed the better part of a silent-screen actor's job. In no time, a casting director noticed the small, attractive teenager and asked Gloria if she would like to appear in a movie. On a lark, she accepted the offer and the next day returned to the studio wearing the same outfit—as requested by the casting director—to play a bit role as a guest in a wedding scene.

Gloria was offered a contract as an extra, and she leapt at the offer. The job would provide her with a good income and, perhaps more important, with an excuse for quitting school, which she detested. At that point, however, Gloria had no overriding ambition to become an actress or a film star. She found the movies "crude and silly" and couldn't bear to watch herself on the screen; but films paid $13.25 a week for what she considered light work. While employed at the Essanay Studios, Gloria, like the other actors, supplied her costumes from her own closet. With no dialogue, it was largely through wardrobe that Gloria began to learn how to project a convincing image on film. She was frequently cast as a thirty-something sophisticated woman, which allowed the teenage actress to dress as maturely as she pleased.

In 1915, Joseph Swanson was notified that he was being transferred to the Philippines. While he went ahead to Manila to set up a home for his wife and daughter, Gloria and her mother decided to take a vacation in California before the overseas journey. Gloria was blasé about having to give up her job at Essanay, since she had never seriously considered making a career of acting. On the train ride west, Addie shocked her daughter with the announcement that she was going to file for divorce. That divorce would transform Gloria's life plan.

The casting director who had originally hired Gloria gave her a letter of introduction to Mack Sennett, then the premier comedic movie director in Hollywood. With her trip to Manila canceled, Gloria decided to introduce herself to Sennett. As she settled into Los Angeles, she noticed that the ubiquitous unemployed actors were, on the whole, badly dressed in garish patterns with an abundance of trims and ruffles. For her meeting with Sennett, she chose what she thought was an elegant ensemble and applied her makeup deliberately. At her interview, Sennett took one look at her and said, "The clothes are terrible and that makeup is a joke. [Show up] on Thursday." Insulted and hurt, Gloria returned to the apartment she was sharing with her mother and refused to go to the studio at her appointed time. The next day, however, a car arrived at her door to pick her up and deliver her to Sennett's movie set. Gloria later learned that what Sennett had objected to at her interview was that she dressed like a thirty-year-old woman rather than the teenager she was. It was her youth Sennett wanted to exploit, not a false maturity.

"Gloria Swanson was wonderful to work with," remembered Clarence Badger, her first director at Sennett's studio. "Even then, in her youthful days, she was most talented, appealing, and charming, definitely possessing screen personality to such an outstanding

Gloria Swanson had her first taste of screen stardom when she appeared in Mack Sennett's romantic comedies.

degree that it was easy to foresee she would go a long way in pictures." Such extraordinary talent did not go unnoticed for long, and Gloria would soon be given the opportunity to display her range in a series of history-making dramatic roles.

While Gloria's movie career was gaining momentum, her personal life took a turn for the worse when she eloped with Wallace Beery, a popular film comedian twelve years her senior. Young and impressionable, Gloria didn't think twice about marrying a man she hardly knew—yet she regretted her impetuous action almost immediately, seeking a separation and eventually a divorce. Disillusioned by her experience with men, Gloria sought to take control of her life and her career. Still, she continued to look for a man to take on some of the responsibility of supporting her, her mother, and eventually her children. Despite six trips to the altar, Gloria never succeeded.

Her skill as an actress, however, was beginning to draw critical acclaim and a steady following of admirers; among them was Cecil B. DeMille, who headed a production team at Paramount Studios. Leaving behind the romantic comedies she made with Sennett, Gloria accepted an offer from DeMille and embarked on a new direction in her career. Gloria's decision to join DeMille would prove to be perhaps the single most fortuitous move in the young actress's career.

DeMille cast Gloria in a series of films that explored the changes in modern American society in the post–World War I era; the director was particularly fond of scripts examining the impact of the developing "modern woman" in male-female relationships. The end of World

In films such as Don't Change Your Husband (below) and Male and Female (left), Gloria's portrayal of a seductive, independent woman captivated audiences. In typical DeMille style, these films included lavish sets and costumes, creating a lush atmosphere that moviegoers found mesmerizing.

would have dwarfed a lesser actress, but Gloria, petite as she was, carried them off with aplomb.

In 1919, not long after she had begun her partnership with DeMille, *The Los Angeles Times* called Gloria Swanson "one of the most talented film stars, [whose] popularity since she joined the DeMille forces exceeds even that of many a star appearing with her company. She has, as a matter of fact, been a sort of fad with young women all over the country, so far as her striking little mannerisms and her particular manner of dressing is concerned, and this is true among the sophisticated fans of the big towns equally with those of the small . . . "

In 1920, Paramount hired Elinor Glyn, a notoriously daring English writer, to prepare a series of film story lines. Her first screenplay, *The Great Moment*, would star Gloria Swanson. At their first meeting, Glyn pronounced Gloria "positively Egyptian" in appearance, and informed the twenty-two-year-old star that she was a favorite of the Prince of Wales (later the Duke of Windsor). Glyn, a fashion trendsetter herself, helped revamp Gloria's style from the over-the-top costumes she sported in the DeMille films to a more streamlined look that favored clean, uncluttered lines. To complete Gloria's transformation to a bona fide glamour queen,

War I saw fundamental shifts in American society; a crumbling class system allowed more freedom of movement among the strata of society. When women won the vote in 1919, images of the ideal American woman began to change, as a younger generation engaged in a wholesale revolt against their parents' Victorian conventions.

To add to the hypnotic sense of fantasy surrounding DeMille's productions, Gloria's offscreen persona had merged in the public's mind with that of her onscreen image. Her exotic looks were a striking contrast to the girlish appearance of America's reigning cinema sweetheart, Mary Pickford, and the subtle, unforced quality of her acting suited the intimacy of the camera, offering a refreshing departure from the stiff, theatrical gestures of some of her peers. Audiences instantly responded to the real-life immediacy Gloria imparted: she created real women, not caricatures.

DeMille recognized that he could draw women into movie theaters by adding a rich assortment of costumes to his films. Gloria was an eager student ready to don any outrageous ensemble, and DeMille clothed her in the finest silks, furs, and real jewels; she wore gowns covered with pearls and costumes with thirty-five-foot trains. The enormous, elaborate headpieces and coiffures he created

Glyn enlisted her personal dressmaker, who created the breathtaking ensembles Gloria would wear offscreen—ensuring a seamless connection between Gloria's film and real-life personae.

In 1923, after working with DeMille for four years, Gloria headed to New York to begin shooting a movie at Paramount's East Coast studio. Hollywood in the early 1920s was still somewhat of a swashbuckling outpost compared with the old East Coast cities, and Gloria delighted in discovering Manhattan's sophistication. A keen observer, she noted with great interest the refined, simple lines of the clothes favored by New York women. Following Elinor Glyn's cue, Gloria embraced the chic New York fashions. The drop-waist styles that emerged in the early 1920s suited Gloria's small frame, which benefited from the elongating effect of the silhouette.

After years of being cast in the roles of wealthy, urbane women, Gloria made a departure in *Manhandled*, in which she played a department-store clerk. In the film, she sported a sleek, bobbed hairstyle that she thought was both appropriate for her role and quite flattering. Convinced that her head was too large, Gloria chose hairstyles and hats that downplayed its size in relation to her body. And the moment Gloria cut her long hair short, of course, women throughout the country followed suit.

By this time, Gloria was the biggest box-office draw in Hollywood; fan magazines had dubbed her the Queen of the Screen. The higher her star climbed, the more money she earned—and the more she spent. In 1924, *Photoplay* magazine published a report of Gloria's expenditures: five thousand dollars on shoes, nine thousand six hundred dollars on silk stockings, six thousand dollars on perfume, five thousand dollars on headdresses, another five thousand dollars on purses and handbags, ten thousand dollars on lingerie, ten thousand dollars on wraps and coats, twenty-five thousand dollars on furs, and fifty thousand dollars on gowns. The one area in which she economized was her jewelry. Rather than purchase expensive gems and baubles, she rented them at ten percent of their cost. One year, she spent five hundred thousand dollars on rented jewelry, the purchase price of which would have amounted to five million dollars.

This lavish lifestyle was in keeping with the high-living and high-spending ways of the Roaring Twenties.

Elinor Glyn (above right), who became young Gloria's mentor, once said, "Motion pictures are going to change everything. They're the most important thing that's come along since the printing press. People don't care about royalty anymore. They're much more interested in queens of the screen, like you, my dear." In the background photo, Gloria displays her royal demeanor.

163

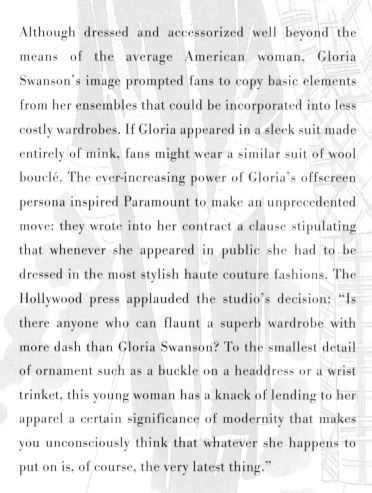

Enthralled by French fashion, Gloria insisted that Coco Chanel design her costumes for the 1931 film Tonight or Never *(left). Sketches of two other Chanel outfits appear in the background. The scene at right, from* What a Widow, *aptly captures the enormous sums Gloria spent on her personal wardrobe.*

Although dressed and accessorized well beyond the means of the average American woman, Gloria Swanson's image prompted fans to copy basic elements from her ensembles that could be incorporated into less costly wardrobes. If Gloria appeared in a sleek suit made entirely of mink, fans might wear a similar suit of wool bouclé. The ever-increasing power of Gloria's offscreen persona inspired Paramount to make an unprecedented move: they wrote into her contract a clause stipulating that whenever she appeared in public she had to be dressed in the most stylish haute couture fashions. The Hollywood press applauded the studio's decision: "Is there anyone who can flaunt a superb wardrobe with more dash than Gloria Swanson? To the smallest detail of ornament such as a buckle on a headdress or a wrist trinket, this young woman has a knack of lending to her apparel a certain significance of modernity that makes you unconsciously think that whatever she happens to put on is, of course, the very latest thing."

In 1925, Gloria left for France, where she became the first actress to shoot a movie entirely on location: *Madame Sans-Gêne*, the Empire-period story of a washerwoman who befriends Napoleon and finds acceptance—and, ultimately, a husband—among elite society. While abroad, Gloria embraced French haute couture, and took special delight in the creations of Chanel and Patou. At the time, Coco Chanel was just beginning to gain renown, revolutionizing female dress with her practical yet stylish clothes. She popularized the "little black dress" as the most suitable evening attire for the modern woman; she also created the two-piece suit, with its coordinating cardigan jacket. Jean Patou shared the spotlight with Chanel in the 1920s, designing clothes that suited women's active lifestyles. The fact that American women inspired Patou artistically made him popular among Hollywood actresses, including Gloria. Her trip to France would complete the evolution of Gloria's personal style—a sophisticated aesthetic that incorporated the reigning tenets of fine couture: a good eye for color, a respect for clean, classic lines, and a highly considered, judicious approach to accessories and embellishments.

On the set of *Madame Sans-Gêne*, Gloria fell in love with her French interpreter, a handsome but impoverished nobleman who went by the almost impossibly aristocratic title of Henri, Marquis Le Bailly de la Falaise de la Coudraye. They began a passionate affair while she was in the midst of divorcing her second husband, Henry Somborn. As the film neared completion, Gloria discovered she was pregnant. By that time, her contract included a morality clause, which studios had begun to insert after a series of sordid Hollywood scandals threatened the industry. Realizing that a child conceived out of wedlock would destroy her career, she chose to have an abortion rather than risk professional and financial ruin. The day after she wed Henri, she underwent the procedure, but the operation was botched and Gloria became terribly ill with blood poisoning. Jubilant headlines celebrating the marriage of Hollywood's greatest star to a member of the European nobility were replaced the next day by shocking stories of Gloria's struggle to survive in a French hospital.

*G*loria Swanson, shown here with her husband Henri, Marquis Le Bailly de la Falaise de la Coudraye, donned men's attire six years before Marlene Dietrich brought her female tuxedo to America.

Gloria managed to recover, and after a period of recuperation, she embarked with Henri for the United States and the premiere of *Madame Sans-Gêne*. When they docked in New York, the newlyweds were met by hysterical fans, thrilled to see their favorite star alive and well and accompanied by her dashing new husband. From the moment the ship arrived in New York harbor until the moment their train reached California, Gloria required police protection to shield her from zealous fans. In Hollywood, the couple was greeted by banners and brass bands. Studio employees, among them future costume designer Edith Head, were summoned to welcome Gloria back to Hollywood by throwing roses at her feet. The ovation overwhelmed Gloria, who realized

the enormous price she had paid to keep her unprecedented acclaim and popularity. Unaware of her personal turmoil, Hollywood continued to idolize her. As one of her directors noted that day, "If Gloria were thirty-five instead of twenty-five, she could run for President. There's no one else like her." Indeed, no performer before her had experienced fame on such a colossal scale. Gloria, however, met the adulation with apprehension. "All that cheering tonight," she said to her mother as they left the Hollywood premiere of *Madame Sans-Gêne*, "had nothing to do with my acting. It was all publicity. They weren't cheering me as an actress. They were only using me to make money. I'm just twenty-six. Where do I go from here?"

Gloria began by leaving the studios and striking out on her own. After spending twelve years bound to one studio after another, her career manipulated by directors and studio executives, Gloria turned down a highly restrictive, million-dollar contract with Paramount. She left behind six years of successful film projects and joined United Artists, the corporation founded by the actors Douglas Fairbanks, Mary Pickford, and Charlie Chaplin. At her new studio, Gloria was required to make only one or two pictures a year as opposed to the mandatory four or more at other studios. She would also be guaranteed a larger income, since she was permitted to invest in other successful United Artists film projects.

In the 1920s, the Motion Picture Producers and Distributors of America was galvanized by complaints from religious leaders and citizens regarding the sex and violence depicted in films. Former postmaster general William Hays was appointed to a regulatory commission that would have the power to censor material deemed inappropriate; he became so powerful in his new role that the production code he initiated soon carried his name. One of the potential film properties that was banned by the Hays code was the hit Broadway play *Rain*, written by John Colton and based on a short story by Somerset Maugham called "Miss Thompson." Gloria thought that the story, which dealt openly with issues of prostitution and religion, was a perfect vehicle for her career. Always a bit rebellious at heart and never afraid to take a risk, Gloria announced she would be filming a movie based on the Maugham short story. Before the censors even made the connection to the banned stage play, *Sadie Thompson* had been shot and edited and was ready to be distributed. The film was a huge success and earned Gloria an Academy Award nomination for Best Actress in the Academy's very first awards ceremony in 1928.

The fate of some other United Artists productions was not as encouraging. One of Gloria's biggest disappointments as a producer was *Queen Kelly*, an unorthodox film about a schoolgirl, abducted by a prince, who eventually becomes the madam of a whorehouse in Africa. The film was Gloria's first extensive collaboration with the temperamental but brilliant director Erich von Stroheim, whose excessive attention to detail drove the project significantly over budget. Gloria had to halt production halfway through the film.

In 1927, talking pictures made their much ballyhooed debut. Although many silent-film actors, including Charlie Chaplin, believed the medium of film would be ruined by this new technology, audiences were thrilled to hear the voices of their favorite performers for the first time. Every actor eventually attempted to make the transition to sound, but not everyone survived the change. While Clara Bow and John Gilbert saw their careers come to an end after their debuts in talking pictures, other actors, notably Gary Cooper, Norma Shearer, and Joan Crawford, enjoyed sudden success. By 1929, Greta Garbo and Gloria Swanson were the only major stars who had yet to make their first talkie. When Gloria's film *The Trespasser* was released that year, audiences and critics were pleasantly surprised: not only could Gloria speak her lines well, but she also displayed a charming singing voice. Permanently dispelling speculation that sound would be the death knell for Gloria's career, *Vanity Fair* happily reported, "A not too credulous audience at the New York premiere rose and cheered as the indomitable and really talented actress talked and sang her way back to screen prestige." She received her second Academy Award nomination for this performance.

Yet despite this latest triumph, Gloria's star in Hollywood was falling. Glamour remained an important part of the formula for movie magic, but audiences, still rebounding from the disastrous effects of the Great Depression, viewed Gloria as a relic of the wanton luxury and excess that had precipitated the stock market crash. Gloria made

A savvy dresser, Gloria knew how to camouflage her flaws. The large fur collar on this gown drew attention to her face and minimized the size of her head.

only seven movies between 1929 and 1941. Refusing to stay in Hollywood as a has-been, she left California in 1938 and settled in New York. Although she had never completed high school, she had an inquisitive mind and was an avid reader. She became involved in several business enterprises during her retirement from film, including a company that made cosmetics from natural ingredients and a clothing company that specialized in designs for women with large figures. She also founded Multiprises, Inc., which helped scientists escape Nazi Germany and market and promote their inventions. For a time, she was even a reporter for UPI, and covered the wedding of Grace Kelly and Prince Rainier.

Then, in 1950, Gloria Swanson made what is still considered the most remarkable comeback in Hollywood history when she accepted Billy Wilder's offer to star in *Sunset Boulevard*. Gloria played Norma Desmond, a faded and deluded silent-film star

who yearns, to the point of dementia, for her screen comeback. Her exceptional performance earned Gloria her final nomination for an Academy Award. Inevitably, there was no shortage of writers and critics quick to draw parallels between the real Gloria and her neurotic character in the film.

Despite the dimming of her career, Gloria herself neither faded nor burned out. For Gloria, glamour had become an important component of her life—something she couldn't simply lay aside. The aura she exuded on the screen was forever woven into her private identity; it remained so until the day she died, in April of 1983.

When Cecil B. DeMille was asked to say a word about Gloria, many years after their film collaboration had ended, he responded simply: "When you put them all together and add them up, Gloria Swanson comes out the movie star of all movie stars. She had something that none of the rest of them had." Gloria Swanson was exotic, she was sensual, she was glamorous, and perhaps more than any other Hollywood performer, she helped American cinema, and American fashion, come of age.

Gloria's Academy Award–nominated role in Sunset Boulevard *(above) resurrected her career, even though she was still a Hollywood legend. Her innate sense of style and chic ensembles (right) mesmerized fans, who found her offscreen image (left) just as fashionable.*

Joan Crawford

In 1944, Joan Crawford feared her career was over. After a two-year absence from the screen, she was eager to find a project that might restore her popularity. After reading the script for *Mildred Pierce*, and recognizing the potential of its title role—a waitress who works her way up in the world only to commit murder to protect her selfish daughter—Joan lobbied hard for the part. She succeeded in convincing the producer, Jerry Wald, that she was perfect for the role; the director, Michael Curtiz, who had recently made his name with *Casablanca*, was a hard sell. "Me direct that temperamental bitch?" he is said to have exploded at Wald. "Not on your goddamn life! She comes over here with her high-hat airs and her goddamn shoulder pads! I won't work with her! She's through. Washed up! Why should I waste my time directing a has-been?" The first day on the set was a disaster. When Joan appeared in her costume, Curtiz erupted: "You and your goddamn shoulder pads. I warned you!" Joan passively retreated, then returned wearing a dress she had purchased that morning at Sears for $2.98—with no padding in the shoulders at all. Curtiz again ranted about her shoulder pads, and began to tear at the dress—only to discover what every wardrobe assistant in Hollywood already knew: Joan Crawford's shoulders were a linebacker's dream.

Today, the collective impression left by Crawford's domineering shoulders, fierce eyebrows, and boldly colored lips has become virtually indistinguishable with the image of Crawford as a wire-hanger-wielding monster: an unfortunate legacy of the book and film *Mommie Dearest*, written by the actress's adopted

Joan Crawford's dramatic makeup and padded shoulders influenced a generation of women—and launched one of the most popular fashion trends of the twentieth century.

daughter, Christina, after Crawford's death in 1977. Whether or not the allegations of abuse are true, our perception of Joan Crawford, one of the most glamorous and popular movie stars of the 1930s, has been tainted. There is poignancy in the knowledge that, from the moment she arrived in Hollywood in 1925—a stocky chorus girl named Lucille Le Sueur—Joan Crawford worked tirelessly to achieve stardom and maintain the adulation of her fans. She never took her fame for granted, and felt an obligation to her fans rarely seen today.

In the early years of Hollywood, as the star system became the guiding principle of the movie industry, major studios began to take great pains to build and meticulously groom their stars for instant recognition. Joan Crawford seemed to have an innate understanding of the image-making process, and without the tutelage of a studio she set out to craft an iconic persona that fans would forever associate with her name. While she toiled as a bit player at MGM, unnoticed by the top management, she experimented with her looks, using as a model the bold makeup and hairstyles of venerated actresses such as Gloria Swanson and Greta Garbo. It was not until the early 1930s, after years of observing the best makeup artists and costume designers in Hollywood, that Joan Crawford arrived at the legendary look for which her name has become a byword: padded shoulders, severely tailored suits, heavily painted eyes, darkly drawn brows, and a wide, brightly colored mouth.

The Joan Crawford look, which found scores of disciples, was not created without the help of a trusted designer. Jackie Kennedy had Oleg Cassini, Gloria Swanson had Chanel and Patou, the Duchess of Windsor had Mainbocher and Schiaparelli, and Joan Crawford had Adrian. One of Hollywood's top costume designers, Adrian was the man responsible for playing up, rather than minimizing, Joan's broad shoulders, creating in the process a potent fashion trend. For the price of a movie ticket—and with a moderate outlay for a Joan Crawford–style knockoff from the local department store—women could buy a piece of Hollywood glamour. The success of this style owed a great deal to Joan's tremendous star power, of course, and her enthralling rags-to-riches life story became an inspiration to women of the 1930s and 1940s still coping with the economic hardships of the Great Depression.

Lucille Fay Le Sueur was born on March 23, 1904, in San Antonio, Texas. When she was still an infant, her father, a day laborer, abandoned his family. Lucille's mother moved with her young son and infant daughter to Lawton, Oklahoma, where she married Harry Cassin, a local vaudeville theater owner. Young Lucille was fascinated by her stepfather's trade and spent much of her time at the theater. The itinerant actors and dancers who performed there befriended the young girl, teaching her, among other things, how to dance and apply stage makeup.

When Lucille Fay was eleven years old, her mother and stepfather divorced. Moving to Kansas City, Missouri, her mother opened a laundry and settled her family into the small, dirty rooms behind the store. Joan was placed in Saint Agnes's convent school, where she had to wait on tables to pay for her room and tuition. Once she had completed her education there, her mother found her a job in an upper-class boarding school for girls, where she would again work to pay for her classes and lodging. Her chores were grueling, and Lucille was often beaten by the woman who ran the school. After graduation, Lucille worked in a local department store selling notions. She was, by all accounts, miserable.

Her only respite was going out dancing in the evenings. She had matured into an attractive young woman with brown hair, large blue eyes, and full lips, and with her youthful exuberance she became quite popular with the boys. When a locally based traveling song-and-dance show came to Kansas City and held auditions, Lucille snuck away during her lunch hour to try out. Five feet four inches tall and stocky, Lucille was not, by most standards, chorus-girl material, but what she lacked in height she made up for in enthusiasm; she was hired to join the troupe. Eventually she made her way to Chicago, where she was seen by noted theatrical promoter J. J. Shubert, who admired her talent for playing to the audience. He offered her a job in New York, and in a matter of weeks Lucille was promoted from the back of the chorus line to the front. In New York, an MGM talent scout named Harry Rapf spotted her, and gave her a screen test. Studio executives were so impressed with Lucille's natural radiance and charisma that they immediately offered her a five-year studio contract.

Twenty-one-year-old Lucille Le Sueur arrived in Hollywood in 1925, during the heyday of silent film, just two years before talking pictures turned Hollywood on its head. The most popular and glamorous star of the day was Gloria Swanson, America's movie monarch. Lucille had not even considered becoming an actress; her primary goal was to be a great dancer and have a good time. When she was placed at the center of the Hollywood star machine, however, she was thrilled at the prospects before her.

After Lucille had played insignificant roles in three films, the head of publicity for MGM decided that the name Lucille Le Sueur, whether it was a real name or not, sounded like a bad stage name. The studio's solution was to hold a nationwide contest in *Movie Weekly*—with a one-thousand-dollar prize—to find a screen name for the new starlet. The two-page article that accompanied the contest rules described Lucille Le Sueur as "the ideal young American girl of today." The name the studio chiefs initially selected was Joan Arden, but they soon discovered that there was already an MGM contract player by that name. The second choice stuck. From the beginning, Lucille hated her stage name, complaining that Crawford sounded too much like "crawfish." None too pleased with her new first name either, for a period of time she asked friends to call her Joann.

Despite a spate of film roles, Lucille, or Joan, still felt underemployed and underappreciated. She wandered the sound stages at MGM, observing the acting techniques of the leading performers. She studied how the women dressed and carried themselves, looking for inspiration for her own hair, makeup, and clothing, hungry for anything that would set her apart from the host of other pretty young hopefuls like herself. One day a camera technician complimented Joan on her fine bone structure, pointing out that if she lost some weight the contours of her face could be more readily captured by the movie camera. Taking the advice to heart, Joan shed twenty pounds from her athletic frame. To get herself noticed, she amiably posed for innumerable publicity shots in sometimes outlandish getups. Naturally, she became a favorite in the publicity department, which showed its appreciation by regularly sending her photos to magazines. "Joan was our first attempt at actually creating a screen personality from scratch," one publicist explained. "She was more ambitious and was, above all else, true to herself. Most stars were glorified puppets who did and said what was dictated to them. Joan had a mind of her own, but she was not excluded from the usual editing or criticism. She was watched very carefully, but her public relations proved to be a Hollywood dream, and the fan magazines' delight."

Working with the studio photographers was an education in itself. The more time Joan spent in front of the camera, the more accomplished she became at posing alluringly and using the effect of artificial lighting to her advantage. She later said of this period, "Lots of newcomers to films undoubtedly think that posing for

This early MGM publicity photo of Joan Crawford displays her youthful exuberance and athleticism.

photos is a waste of time. It doesn't need to be. I have made a careful study of every single still picture that was ever shot of me. I wanted these stills to teach me what not to do on the screen. I scrutinized the grin on my face, my hairdo, my posture, my makeup, the size of my feet."

Every evening, Joan was out on the town, at premieres and dance parties. Young, ambitious, good-looking, and endowed with boundless energy, she personified a generation of young women who cut their hair, shortened their skirts, and seemed to take pleasure in flouting the conventions of their staid predecessors. In the 1920s, as waistlines dropped to the hips, hemlines crept to unheard-of heights. This more liberating style of dress, in turn, required a new approach to undergarments, which became lighter and more comfortable. Coverage, however, was still of paramount concern, since young women danced the Charleston and other raucous dances with abandon, letting their skirts twirl up in the air, exposing the knee and sometimes even a little thigh.

With her limited education and a dearth of cultural refinement, Joan lived large—she laughed the loudest, danced the longest, and played the hardest. Her style of dress at the time reflected her lack of experience; she mistook overdone, gaudy dresses for high fashion. "In my early days in Hollywood I was so covered with ruffles, bows and spangles that you could hardly notice me," she later recalled in her memoir *My Way of Life*. "I plucked my eyebrows to a little line and drew a tiny little cupid's bow for a mouth. Off-screen, when I was dancing every night, my skirts were a little too short, my heels a little too high, and my hair a little too frizzy and a little too bright. I wore brilliant red nail polish when everybody else wore pink, and when it was the thing to be fair I got a deep suntan. I loved being in the vanguard—and I was. They all followed along behind. This was the era when everybody wanted to be the complete flapper, to be noticed, to dance faster than anybody else."

Joan was able to indulge her love for dancing when she was given the starring role in *Our Dancing Daughters* (1928), a film that examined the impact of the Jazz Age on the younger generation. Flush with her first lead role, and stylishly dressed by Adrian, Joan Crawford

*J*oan's breakout role in the
silent film Our Dancing Daughters
(left) captured the flamboyant
American spirit of the Jazz Age—
an era dominated by the energetic
Charleston (above), speakeasies,
and shorter skirts.

leapt from mild notoriety to stardom. F. Scott Fitzgerald, who knew something about 1920s decadence himself, said, "Joan Crawford is doubtless the best example of the flapper . . . a young thing with a talent for living." *Our Dancing Daughters* was a huge hit, and virtually overnight Joan Crawford's face and form insinuated themselves into the American consciousness. Women copied her hair, her clothes, and her makeup. The fan mail started pouring into the studio, and Joan, with almost superhuman diligence, personally answered each letter she received. Thus began the most important long-term relationship of her life: the bond between her and her fiercely devoted fans. She never tired of reminding herself that, if not for her fans, she would be back in Kansas City working as a sales clerk. Joan reciprocated this devotion by never, ever failing to dress the part of the star—obsessively maintaining a glamorous demeanor for any and every public appearance.

Around the same time her film career was taking off, Joan met Douglas Fairbanks, Jr., scion of a Hollywood dynasty that included his stepmother, Mary Pickford. Joan and Douglas fell in love quickly and were soon married. Fairbanks had sophisticated tastes and manners, and Joan tempered her brassy style to please him and her in-laws. She dressed more conservatively, setting aside her loud colors and short skirts. She dyed her flashy red hair a more subdued auburn. She toned down her raucous laugh and chatter and made an effort to converse in more ladylike tones. She and Fairbanks became the most popular couple in Hollywood. Reports of the storybook marriage filled magazines and newspapers, for which the couple happily furnished interviews and intimate glances into their Hollywood home. While both of them shrewdly recognized the value of courting publicity, life under the relentless scrutiny of reporters began to overwhelm them. To add to the friction mounting between them, it was widely acknowledged that Joan's career was soaring faster than her husband's. In 1933, after four years of marriage, Joan Crawford and Douglas Fairbanks divorced.

While some actresses seemed aloof and distant, Joan Crawford, beneath all her sexy costumes, displayed an earthy quality that allowed women to identify with her.

In the late 1920s, talking pictures began to replace silent films, and Joan Crawford was one of the few performers in Hollywood, along with the Barrymores, Gloria Swanson, Gary Cooper, and Norma Shearer, to successfully make the transition to sound. Audiences were pleased when they heard Joan's deep, husky voice; it suited her sensual screen presence. Nonetheless, Joan eventually hired a voice and diction coach, recognizing that if she wanted to play sophisticated women on the screen she had to sound the part.

By the early 1930s, Joan Crawford was one of the biggest stars in Hollywood. Candid biographical profiles appeared in the press, as Hollywood set out to add a mythic quality to Joan's life. American women, hooked by the glamour, were positively enraptured by Joan's rags-to-riches story. Before the eyes of a nation, Joan was making a cinematic and real-life transition from daring flapper to independent, successful woman. She was one of the leading actresses in what were then called "women's films"—movies specifically intended to attract female audiences. The fan magazine *Motion Picture* unabashedly told readers, "If Lucille Le Sueur could acquire Joan Crawford's glamour in a few short years, there is hope for you and You and YOU!"

Nineteen thirty-two was a significant year for Joan. The style she had been looking for since arriving in Hollywood, and that she had fine-tuned during her marriage to Fairbanks, finally moved onscreen in three major films: *Grand Hotel*, *Rain*, and *Letty Lynton*. In both *Grand Hotel* and *Rain*, Joan played working-class women in roles that frankly addressed moral and sexual issues and that required a seductive appearance. She decided to break away from the thin, heavily plucked eyebrows and heart-shaped lips that had defined her look up until then. As the 1930s wore on, Joan enhanced her naturally shapely mouth with makeup, making it appear progressively wider and more square. The look

For her roles as a prostitute in Grand Hotel *(background) and* Rain *(below), Joan devised a new look for herself that she felt was in keeping with her character. "I felt that a more sensuous look was needed," she later wrote, "Definite features were called for, and I found that I liked the look so much I kept it."*

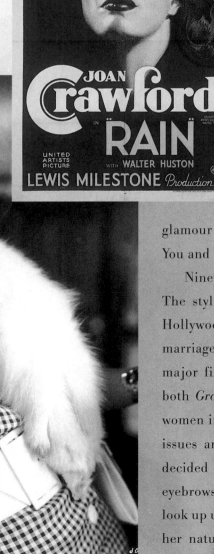

caught on not only with average women, but also with other stars: Gloria Swanson, Katharine Hepburn, and Marlene Dietrich all began to subscribe to this new aesthetic. The look remained identified with Joan for the rest of her life, although in her later years it took on a hard, studied appearance consonant with the stylized roles that came at the end of her otherwise luminous career.

It was not until later in 1932, with the release of *Letty Lynton*, that Joan Crawford truly strengthened her grip on American fashion. Joan had been working with

Adrian for some time, and the designer had grown familiar with Joan's unusually broad-shouldered figure. After their first meeting, Adrian had reportedly referred to Joan as a "female Johnny Weissmuller." Faced with the dilemma of such a distinctive physique, Adrian had arrived at an inspired solution: instead of trying to hide Joan's shoulders, he would accentuate them—even celebrate them. In the waning years of the flapper era, the boxy, drop-waisted style that characterized women's fashions was replaced by yet another new silhouette. The waistline slowly crept up from the hips and returned to its natural place on the torso, and the bias cut, introduced by French couturier Madeleine Vionnet, began to enjoy looser, more flamboyant interpretations. In the early 1930s, women's dresses began once again to emphasize the curves of the female figure. In order to accentuate the smallness of the waist and counterbalance the curve of the hips, a broader shoulder line was introduced in the late 1920s. By the early 1930s, French couturiers were featuring an extended shoulder line, but the style was not catching on with American women.

What French couturiers had been unable to achieve over a period of years, Adrian did in one fell swoop. The dress that defined the new Joan Crawford was a white, starched organdy gown with ruffled shoulders and a flared skirt. The dress featured what would become Joan's most famous look: wide, padded shoulders that made the hips look extraordinarily slim. The gown was an overnight sensation; women flocked to their hometown stores looking for dresses with puffed or ruffled shoulders and sleeves. The impact of Adrian's design was immediately apparent to costume designers in Hollywood. Edith Head, costume designer at Paramount, called the *Letty Lynton* dress the single most important influence on fashion since the advent of the motion picture. Walter Plunkett, the costume designer for *Gone With the Wind*, summarized the genesis of Adrian's creation: "Paris had padded shoulders before Adrian took them. He was very smart. They had just come out in Paris and weren't very important yet, but Adrian saw their possibilities. And he saw them particularly as,

In 1932, Joan Crawford appeared in Letty Lynton, *introducing a look that would captivate women for a decade.*

'What the hell do you do with a woman that has shoulders as broad as Joan Crawford's? Take this new fashion of pads, make them even bigger and set a fashion with them.'" Even French couturier Elsa Schiaparelli, one of the earliest proponents of an enlarged shoulder line, had to admit, "The film fashions of today are your fashions of tomorrow."

Department stores like Macy's carried less elaborate copies of the *Letty Lynton* dress in their Cinema Shop, a department that specialized in movie costumes copied for the ready-to-wear market. Pattern companies such as Butterick as well as movie magazines provided patterns so that the average middle-class woman could make her own *Letty Lynton*-inspired dress. Manufacturers and merchants followed the Macy's lead and began featuring styles that were borrowed from or inspired by the costumes that appeared in the movies.

Throughout the ensuing decade, Adrian would design both Joan's screen costumes and her personal wardrobe. The fashion for padded shoulders that had been initiated in 1932 would remain dominant well into the 1940s, and would be revived from time to time thereafter, most notably in the 1980s, when TV's *Dynasty*, featuring Linda Evans as Krystal Carrington, brought the extended shoulder line back into vogue.

Soon Adrian streamlined Joan's look, putting her in crisply tailored suits, still with padded shoulders, and in skirts that fit smoothly over the hips. But once Adrian had created what she saw as her definitive look, Joan Crawford was never comfortable in any other style, having lost much of the flair for experimentation that carried her through her early twenties. She believed that this was

In their 1933 spring catalog, Sears Roebuck featured a dress in the Letty Lynton *style as "the alluring kind of dress that flashes across the screen on your favorite movie star!"*

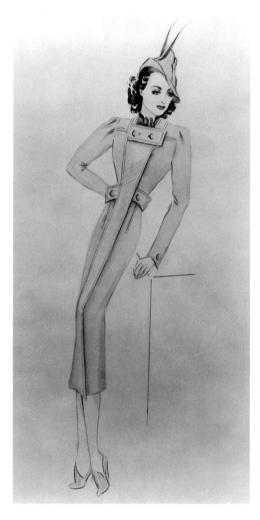

Joan's screen wardrobe included the famous Letty Lynton *dress (left) and the tailored designs by Adrian shown in the sketch above.*

the look that her fans identified as hers; she owed it to them to maintain it. Over the years she would make modifications to her style, in deference to prevailing fashion trends, but Adrian's initial design remained her look for the rest of her life.

In 1937, after nearly a decade as one of the biggest stars in Hollywood, Joan Crawford was named the first Queen of the Movies in *Life* magazine. From 1932 through 1936, she had been one of the top box-office draws in the country and was named The Most Imitated Woman in the World in 1932 and 1937. But in the late 1930s, Joan made a series of films that were financial and critical failures. In 1938, the *Independent Film Journal* hastily branded Joan Crawford, along with Mae West, Greta Garbo, Katharine Hepburn, Marlene Dietrich, and Fred Astaire as "box-office poison." Crawford might have taken pleasure in

While Joan's film career would continue for another eleven years, it never again reached the heights she had achieved in the 1930s. However, in her public and private life Joan could still play her part to the hilt. Her role as a celebrity became increasingly important in her later years. After two more unsuccessful marriages, and after adopting four children, Joan's last marriage, to Albert Steele, the president of Pepsi-Cola, provided a boost to her then-flagging place in the public eye. She threw herself into the promotion of her husband's company, zealously making appearances and speeches as if she were publicizing her latest film project. Joan's glorious run as corporate wife ended in 1959, when Steele died of a heart attack.

Somewhere along the line, pudgy Lucille Le Sueur from Kansas City was permanently subsumed by the larger-than-life persona created at MGM—and Joan Crawford seemed perfectly happy with the transformation. She always played to her fans, was kind and supportive to photographers, and never left home without the perfect makeup, coiffure, and clothes. "I love being a celebrity," she once admitted. "I never go out on the street unless I expect and anticipate and hope and pray that I'll be recognized. That someone will ask for my autograph. When they do, I'm prepared and ready and as well dressed as I possibly can be. And when somebody says, 'There's Joan Crawford,' I say, 'It sure is!'"

the company she was named with, but was nevertheless terribly hurt by the attack; she feared that, as an actress approaching her late thirties, she would be offered fewer film roles just as her studio contract was coming up for renewal. As if to confirm her fears, Louis B. Mayer dealt a further blow to Joan's low morale by offering her a renewal of only one year. Terrified of losing her income and the only job she knew, she settled for a five-year contract at a greatly reduced salary; MGM continued to cast her in mediocre films and dreary roles. In 1943, after eighteen years at the studio, Joan Crawford asked to be released. Warner Brothers offered her a contract, but things weren't any better there. She was disappointed to discover that she was being handed scripts that the studio's premier actress, Bette Davis, had turned down. Then, just as talk began circulating that Joan's career was over, she landed the title role in *Mildred Pierce*, for which she was awarded her only Oscar. The American dream that Crawford had been living since her early triumph in silent films was capped by a history-making comeback.

"She was the perfect image of the movie star, and . . . largely the creation of her own indomitable will."

—George Cukor

Katharine Hepburn

Katharine Hepburn never quite fit into the colossal publicity machine that drove the Hollywood star system. While all around her young starlets painted their faces and donned their brightest ribbons and bows for the publicity-department photographers, Katharine Hepburn—with a nod to the nonconformist ethic her parents had instilled in her—quietly put on a pair of khaki trousers, a dark turtleneck, and a man's dress shirt. With remarkable poise and stout resolve, she single-handedly broke down the dress codes that had kept women confined to skirts for centuries. And while she certainly was a source of frustration for conservative studio executives, never was she an outcast or a pariah. Indeed, Katharine Hepburn reigned as one of Hollywood's most adored and venerated figures—living proof that in a universe of pretty pictures and bright lights, a woman of substance could not only survive but could also thumb her nose at the system and shine as one of that system's brightest and most enduring stars.

Katharine Hepburn's style was viewed as eccentric when she arrived in Hollywood in the 1930s. Today it is celebrated as the quintessential classic American look.

Katharine Houghton Hepburn was born in Hartford, Connecticut, on May 12, 1907, the second child and oldest daughter of Thomas Hepburn and Katharine Houghton. Her parents were mavericks. "The single most important thing anyone needs to know about me," Katharine once said, "is that I am totally, completely the product of two damn fascinating individuals who happened to be my parents. I've had a pretty remarkable life, but compared to my mother and father, I'm dull." Her father was a surgeon who built a

184

children; Katharine is said to have learned to use her fists in the schoolyard. It is not surprising, though, that the girl grew up with few apprehensions about expressing herself freely. Surrounded by brothers until her first sister arrived when she was nine years old, Katharine, or Kathy, as she was called by her family, became a consummate tomboy. She was a natural, fearless athlete, prone to stunts and feats of daring.

At an early age, Katharine realized that the best way to keep up with her brothers was to discard her dresses and petticoats and don their hand-me-downs. Family legend has it that when she attempted to wear her brother Tom's clothes to school, her teacher sent her home to change, considering her attire unsuitable for a young lady. The next day, Katharine showed up for school wearing pants again, and once more she was sent home to change. She returned to school, unchanged, later that day, accompanied by her mother, who informed the teacher, "You don't tell my daughter how to dress. That is my concern, not yours." With the unwavering support of her parents, Katharine never had second thoughts about the propriety of her wardrobe.

When Katharine was thirteen years old, she suffered the first major loss in her life. She and Tom went with their mother on a short trip to stay with a friend of the family in New York, as a reward for their good marks in school. After a few days, their mother returned to Hartford, and Tom and Katharine were permitted to stay a little longer. The morning that they were scheduled to take the train back to Connecticut, Tom didn't come down for breakfast. When Katharine went up to see what was keeping him, she made a gruesome discovery—sometime during the night, Tom had committed suicide by hanging himself. Katharine immediately attempted to free him, but had arrived too late. Katharine was devastated, and her family, always willing to discuss volatile topics, fell completely silent, leaving Katharine to deal with her grief privately. She was unwilling to return to school, and was tutored at home until she left for college. She tried to take her brother's place in the family, assuming his birth date as her own and even contemplating a career in medicine, as her father had wished Tom to do.

Three years later, she left home to attend her mother's alma mater, Bryn Mawr College, in Pennsylvania. She

successful practice and helped found the American Social Hygiene Association, an organization devoted to increased awareness of venereal disease. Her mother, whose family owned Corning Glass, was a Bryn Mawr graduate with a master's degree from Radcliffe. She became president of the Connecticut Women's Suffrage Association and was an early proponent of birth control; she cofounded, along with Margaret Sanger, the organization that eventually became Planned Parenthood.

While the suffrage movement had gained momentum in the early years of the twentieth century, subjects related to sexuality remained strictly taboo. A good number of the Hepburns' neighbors in Hartford were unsettled by the couple's penchant for discussing controversial subjects in polite society. Many parents refused to let their children associate with young Katharine and her five siblings. While such condemnation may have driven other families into conformity, the Hepburns were comfortable with their status as outsiders and encouraged their children to stand up for their convictions. This is not to say that growing up was easy for the Hepburn was hesitant the first time she entered the student dining room, as she would have to sit among strangers, and came into the room haltingly, wearing a bright blue flared skirt, which buttoned down the front, and a blue-and-white Icelandic sweater. Suddenly a student called out, "Self-conscious beauty!" Katharine was mortified by the attention and giggles her entrance had garnered. She went in, ate her meal, and didn't return to the dining room for the rest of the school year.

Although Katharine Hepburn struggled at first to fit in at Bryn Mawr, she soon began to embrace the freedom that girls of the 1920s were enjoying as a younger, middle-class demographic began to alter the country's social fabric. Katharine adopted the lifestyle of the flapper, sneaking out to Philadelphia at night and socializing with local boys—much of the time with a pair named Jack Clarke and Ludlow Ogden Smith, who owned a cottage off campus. Katharine's late-night escapades, among them bathing naked in the school fountain, left little time for schoolwork. Added to her wild behavior was a most unorthodox mode of dress, which owed nothing to her mother's influence and everything to her father's. Dr. Hepburn limited the contents of his closet to two pairs of shoes and two suits and considered anyone with a larger wardrobe a fop. In keeping with this principle, Katharine kept a rather small wardrobe at college, but unlike her father, who favored a crisp, buttoned-down look, Katharine leaned toward worn, baggy men's trousers, oversized sweaters, and roomy men's shirts. Although women's fashion of the 1920s is often described as boyish because of its curve-obscuring, breast-flattening designs, most women considered Katharine's wholesale embrace of men's clothes extreme.

During her freshman year, after a dismal performance in chemistry, Katharine concluded that the medical profession would be better off without her. Finally freed from the burden of following in her father's footsteps, she began to contemplate a career of her own choosing. Having witnessed her mother's success at tending both to career and family, Katharine decided to become an actress. Unsure how her loved ones would greet the news, however, she kept her plans to herself, and set her sights on joining the college varsity dramatic group.

Although she appears here as a proper young woman, with a delicate string of pearls, Katharine typically sported an unconventional look during her college days.

Soon, Katharine limited all her extracurricular activities to the dramatic arts, performing in a number of college productions. Shortly before her graduation, she starred in *The Woman in the Moon*, a play put on as part of the campus May Day festivities. Her performance impressed her friend Jack Clarke, who happened to know a theatrical producer in Baltimore; he offered to provide Katharine with a letter of introduction. Katharine recalled a piece of advice her father had given her: if you want something badly enough, don't send a letter; go in person and make your argument. It's harder to turn someone down, her father would say, when you're staring him in the face (a technique Katharine would also use on studio executives). Letter of introduction in hand, Katharine borrowed a friend's car and arrived unannounced at the Baltimore office of Edwin H. Knopf, who was polite but cool and asked Katharine to contact him again after her graduation. A few days before the ceremony, Katharine eagerly returned to Baltimore, where she found Knopf in the middle of rehearsals. She sat in the back of the theater for hours, waiting for him to walk past so she would have an opportunity to talk with him again. Her patience paid off; Knopf eventually noticed her and told her to show up for rehearsals in a week for a small part in his next production, *The Czarina*. Having secured a professional job in the theater, Katharine realized with great dread that she would have to tell her parents of her intention to become an actress.

She broke the news as the family drove back to Connecticut after graduation. While her mother would have been pleased with any career she chose, Katharine's father was furious. He thought actors were a vain and frivolous lot who took to the stage only to get attention. In spite of his disappointment in her, Katharine returned to Baltimore to begin her life as an actress. With no training other than that of the amateur theatrics at Bryn Mawr, she was particularly fortunate to be taken under the wings of two skilled professionals in the company. Mary Boland, a stage and silent-film actress who was starring as Catherine the Great in *The Czarina*, taught Katharine how to apply stage makeup, while Kenneth MacKenna, another actor in the troupe, took Katharine aside and gave her the name of a voice and acting coach in New York who could help her perfect her technique.

Once her job in Baltimore ended, Katharine set out for New York. In typical Hepburn fashion, Katharine burst into the office of Frances Robinson-Duff, one of the leading acting teachers of the day, and announced she wanted to take lessons. Robinson-Duff overlooked Katharine's brusque manner and agreed to take her on. In New York, Katharine had a knack for constantly finding work. Having seen how the young hopefuls dressed to the nines to get the attention of producers and directors, Katharine decided to go in the other direction. Androgynous appearance notwithstanding, Katharine was a uniquely attractive woman, with a rosy complexion, red hair, and bright blue eyes. She had a slim build that made her five-foot-seven-inch frame seem even taller. As she wrote in her autobiography, "Lest they think that I was making any effort, I used to get myself up in a sort of slouch costume. I had an old stocking cap . . . or no hat in a day of hats. And an old green tweed coat. I would pin the coat together with a safety pin. Throw a sweater over my shoulders; string my hair a bit . . . Very casual for those days. I wanted to look as though it were really nothing to me if I got the part or didn't." While her ruse may have worked as an attention-getter, it was her raw skill in auditions that helped her land part after part, even though her temperament and uneven performances caused her to lose most of her jobs in short order.

Perhaps weary of the roller-coaster ride in New York, in a short-lived flash of conservatism Katharine decided to give up acting and accepted the proposal of a beau from her Bryn Mawr days. Ludlow Ogden Smith came from a well-to-do Philadelphia family and had adored Katharine throughout college. When she moved to New York, he was working there and they continued to see one another. On December 12, 1928, Ludlow and Katharine drove up to her parents' house in Hartford, where they were married by her grandfather. For the occasion, she put aside her masculine attire and donned a white dress of crushed velvet, trimmed with gold embroidery at the neck and sleeves. After a honeymoon in Bermuda, the newlyweds set about house-hunting near Philadelphia; almost immediately, however, Katharine realized that she couldn't put aside her ambition and assume domestic responsibilities. Ludlow was understanding and agreed to return to New York, where the marriage grew increasingly one-sided—with Ludlow displaying greater love and devotion to his wife than she was able to return.

In 1932, after four years of trying to make it on the Broadway stage, Katharine Hepburn had her first taste of success with a starring role in the comedy *The Warrior's Husband*. At the time, Broadway was filled with Hollywood talent scouts eager to tap New York's pool of acting talent for a film industry flush with the success of the talking picture. Word of this bright young newcomer spread from Broadway to Hollywood, where Katharine went to do a screen test. Director George Cukor liked what he saw and offered her a part in *A Bill of Divorcement*. Katharine accepted a contract for one picture at the almost unheard-of fee of fifteen hundred dollars a week.

Representatives from the studio caught their first glimpse of Katharine Hepburn in the flesh when she arrived at the train station in California, wearing a Quaker-blue silk ensemble she had purchased from New York designer Elizabeth Hawes. The outfit consisted of a long flared skirt and a high-necked blouse with a ruffled collar, and was worn with a matching pancake hat and a coat cut like a nineteenth-century riding garment. When she met Cukor later that day, he was amused by her arty and eccentric ensemble. The first order of business was to send her to the studio hairstylist; Katharine may have been personally opposed to primping, but her look was simply not suitable for movies. While he encouraged her

to maintain a more polished look for his film, Cukor nevertheless admired Katharine's angular features and idiosyncratic appearance, and endeavored to make sure that in making her more glamorous he would not extinguish the spark he had seen light up her screen test.

Katharine Hepburn's movie debut was a stunning success. Her dazzling interpretation of a young woman coping with her mentally ill father thrilled critics and audiences. The *London Daily Telegraph* wrote of her performance, "Miss Hepburn has many limitations. She is not at all beautiful, and her voice is uncommonly harsh, though, thank heaven, not shrill. But give her ten minutes to work her spell and you forget these things. You realize that here is something new and different—a very young actress with the power of a well-trained

The Hollywood Reporter *wrote about Katharine after her screen debut in* A Bill of Divorcement: *"The dynamic way in which this newcomer swept the audience off its feet . . . is only a forerunner of the way she will capture followers by the millions."*

tragedienne, a strange, dynamic and moving young person in a profession full of characterless, synthetic blondes."

Following the box-office success of *A Bill of Divorcement*, Katharine was offered a new contract at RKO. Over the next year and a half, she would make five films; her performance in her third, *Morning Glory*, earned Katharine her first Academy Award. Sudden success, though, had not shaken Katharine's steadfast commitment to her unusual personal style. Naturally, Hollywood was appalled at the casual manner in which she dressed. Although she posed for the required publicity stills, she remained completely unseduced by the trappings of glamour that other stars coveted. She never wore makeup unless she was working, preferring a scrubbed-clean look enhanced only occasionally by a little lipstick. At best, Hollywood society found her wardrobe of tailored pants and shirts bizarre.

The many facets of Katharine Hepburn are seen in these shots from the film Morning Glory—*at left, Katharine relaxes in blue jeans on the set with director Lowell Sherman; above, she wears a sophisticated outfit in a publicity photograph.*

Ironically, while Katharine Hepburn was being lambasted for adopting menswear, Marlene Dietrich was winning accolades for donning trousers and creating sex appeal in her mannish suits. The difference was quite simple: Dietrich played the Hollywood game, while Hepburn bucked the system.

Katharine's scandalous decision to wear pants in public was made against a more complicated historical backdrop than most people realize. Trousers, of course, had been a staple of the male wardrobe for hundreds and hundreds of years; then, in the mid-nineteenth century, a small group of women began to stake their claim to this masculine item of apparel. As part of the dress reform movement, women began advocating a female costume that incorporated trousers as a way of freeing their legs from the encumbering layers of obligatory petticoats. While bloomers, as these early female pants were called, were short-lived, they set a valuable precedent. The most notable descendants of the bloomers appeared in the late nineteenth century in the form of sportswear—mainly bathing suits and cycling costumes—that incorporated the bloomer style. By the 1920s, the sight of a woman in trousers was not terribly scandalous in itself, provided that they were worn exclusively around the house. It was only later that the trend toward female trousers gained momentum, when women working in factories during World War II were compelled for safety reasons to wear pants.

Katharine Hepburn's opinion on equality in dress became notorious in Hollywood, and there were numerous accounts of her spirited arguments with studio brass. In one particularly memorable—and possibly apocryphal—episode, the studio management (in one version, RKO, in another, MGM) insisted that Katharine cease wearing pants on the studio lot. When she continued, they stole the pants right out of her dressing room. She vowed that unless they were returned she would simply elect to wear nothing at all. When the studio executives called her bluff, the story goes, Katharine boldly stepped out of her dressing room clad only in silk underpants. In no time her pants were returned, and nothing more was said on the subject. Unlike most stars, who griped endlessly about the intrusiveness of studio policies but did little to challenge them, Katharine Hepburn backed up her convictions with action.

In spite of a general resistance to the more extreme elements of Katharine's personal wardrobe, female moviegoers began to pay close attention to what Katharine Hepburn wore onscreen. When she appeared

The fact that Katharine Hepburn wore trousers or jeans regularly in public, as seen in this photograph, was viewed as an affront to good taste.

Of course, what was viewed as extreme eccentricity in the 1930s is considered classic Hollywood style today, and has been embraced on and off for years by style-conscious actresses and fashion designers. As attractive and athletic dancers "jump and jive" in Gap's stylishly produced ad for khaki pants, they coincidentally celebrate the actress from New England who bravely adopted these tailored clothes as part of her own distinctive look.

In 1934, Katharine Hepburn went to Mexico to obtain a divorce from her husband, Ludlow. Their marriage had begun to disintegrate when Katharine went to California in 1932, and things only worsened as her career progressed and she realized, with some guilt, that she had been using a man who cared deeply for her. Meanwhile, RKO continued to try to make Katharine conform to their ideal vision of a glamorous movie star, and she

in *Holiday* wearing a stark black dress with a scarf pinned to the shoulder, women across the country followed suit. After she appeared in the costume epic *Mary of Scotland,* women incorporated little ruffs and beret-style hunting caps into their own wardrobes. And when she starred as Tracy Lord in *The Philadelphia Story,* dressed by Hollywood's preeminent designer, Adrian, her full-length afternoon gown, which featured a flounced gingham skirt, helped increase the popularity of gingham all over the country for everything from bathing suits to daytime dresses. It would take time, however, for Katharine's unusual choice of personal apparel to catch on—which it ultimately did after World War II, when women began to accept widespread changes in casual dress.

As did those of other female movie stars of the 1930s, Katharine Hepburn's onscreen wardrobes inspired fashion trends. Unlike her contemporaries, however, Katharine had an offscreen style that remained distinctly her own—simple and unencumbered—in contrast to the dazzling look she displayed in films such as Holiday *and* Mary of Scotland.

*D*ressed exquisitely by Adrian, Katharine's youthful,
stylish costumes for The Philadelphia Story *delighted*
female fans and revived her career.

continued to take pleasure in refusing to do so. While she did excellent work in a number of good movies in later years, she suffered a series of terrible flops in the late 1930s and was branded, along with Joan Crawford and Marlene Dietrich, "box-office poison." While Crawford had been deeply wounded by the attack, Hepburn found it all rather amusing and even had a playful argument with Marlene Dietrich over who was the bigger bomb at the box office. Uninspired by the bland scripts RKO was offering, Katharine bought out the remainder of her contract and returned to New York. There, she began rehearsing a play that had been written especially for her by Philip Barry, called *The Philadelphia Story.* She was so pleased with the work that she bought the rights to it; if Hollywood came calling, it would have to negotiate directly with her. The play

was the biggest success of the 1939 Broadway season, and soon MGM was knocking at her door to make the movie version. Katharine's only demand was that she play Tracy Lord, the role she had created on the stage, a spoiled rich girl who matures into a thoughtful woman

The film Woman of the Year *was Katharine's first collaboration with Spencer Tracy, and their legendary onscreen chemistry in eight films delighted moviegoers for twenty-five years.*

executives, but it was precisely the toned-down, timeless nature of her look that helped sustain her in Hollywood well beyond middle age, when the careers of most actresses fade. Viewed primarily as a great actress rather than a great beauty, Katharine Hepburn has enjoyed a rich and varied career, blissfully free of the mediocre parts in B movies that marred the later careers of contemporaries such as Joan Crawford. She has starred in more than forty films and television movies, received a record twelve Academy Award nominations, and won an unprecedented four Oscars for Best Actress—three of them awarded after her sixtieth birthday. And, in 1986, Katharine added to her astonishing list of accolades a lifetime achievement award from the Council of Fashion Designers of America, in recognition of her role as a nonconformist in modern fashion.

While the persona most actors present to their public becomes dated over time, from the very beginning Katharine Hepburn has been identified with the modern feminist woman. George Cukor, her close friend and one of her favorite directors, once said of her, "[Katharine is] a person whose rare charm and strength is her uncompromising individuality . . . From the beginning, Miss Hepburn chose a direct line and stuck to it. It can frankly be said that Hepburn has not grown up to Hollywood. Hollywood has grown up to her."

on the eve of her second marriage. The film was an enormous success, garnering Academy Award nominations for Katharine and her costars, Cary Grant and Jimmy Stewart. Stewart, as it turned out, was the only one of the three to win.

Two years later, Katharine starred with Spencer Tracy in *Woman of the Year*, inaugurating one of the most famous screen partnerships in movie history. While their offscreen romance was kept hidden from the public because of Tracy's wife and family, the relationship was the most important one in Katharine's life. Spencer Tracy was one of the few men for whom Katharine would make concessions, even including adding a little finesse to her trousers and suits so they would be more flattering to her figure. Katharine would remain devoted to Tracy until his death, shortly after the two finished shooting *Guess Who's Coming to Dinner* in 1967.

Katharine's refusal to maintain a conventionally glamorous offscreen image may have angered studio

With her well-tailored, self-confident style, Katharine Hepburn defined a new notion of Hollywood glamour.

Women
Next M

of the
llennium

F

ashion, once the exclusive domain of the wealthy and well-connected, has in recent years become a mass obsession, pursued by millions and fueled by the cult of celebrity. The once clear categories of glamour, elegance, and fame have been blurred, as has the boundary between the fashion and entertainment industries—with new styles emerging not so much as trends but as reflections of a particular star's signature look. Our entertainment media has responded by devoting an extraordinary amount of coverage to the subject of fashion. Tabloid magazines and television shows regularly feature fashion-conscious celebrities. Taking their cue from music videos, film and music award shows typically open with a rapid-fire series of images, as glowing stars arrive on the red carpet in their best borrowed finery, parading on a celebrity version of the haute-couture catwalk. Indeed, it didn't take long for couture designers to recognize the immense marketing potential of putting a highly recognizable star—as opposed to a supermodel—into their clothes. And in an industry in which talent and content are often ignored in the face of dazzling beauty, a star's current project is frequently overshadowed by the look he or she is sporting. Television audiences, hungry for fashion news, watch the pre-Oscar interviews mainly to see whose designs the nominees are wearing.

Perhaps nowhere has the interdependence of fashion and celebrity been brought into sharper relief than in the extraordinary series of recent celebrity estate auctions; they have featured the personal effects of some of the most famous figures of the twentieth century, among them Jacqueline Kennedy Onassis, the Duke and

In the late twentieth century, the symbiotic relationship between designers and entertainers has created potent, recognizable images. Pictured at left is Madonna's provocative cone-shaped corset designed by Jean-Paul Gaultier for her "Express Yourself" video.

197

highlighted the Clintons' shared strengths, the American press and public, accustomed to more traditional First Ladies, did not warm to the notion of Hillary playing such an integral role in her husband's presidency. She was certainly not the first presidential spouse to provide advice and guidance to her husband, but the Clinton administration showed unprecedented candor in illuminating the First Lady's pivotal role in policy decisions.

Despite the significance of Hillary's efforts to help enact change in government, the media focused instead on her perceived lack of style. Besieged by criticism of her hair and wardrobe for most of her two terms in the White House, Hillary Clinton began to experiment with her appearance. As a woman who had made her career a priority long before she encountered celebrity, she appeared uncomfortable with the scrutiny her public persona began to attract. Perhaps the ultimate irony is that Hillary, who has been accused of being "fashion-challenged," is the only First Lady so far to be featured on the cover of *Vogue*, which carried an accompanying article championing her spirit and indomitable will. The editors, with a graceful nod to this independent woman, allowed her to pose in her own clothes.

Jackie Kennedy's continuing resonance as the definitive American fashion icon is due partly to a number of other social and cultural factors. The 1960s witnessed the coming of age of the baby boomer generation, which became a prime consumer of fashion and popular music. Emerging designers such as Mary Quant and Rudi Gernreich tapped into this youthful market, turning away from the older women who had been haute couture's traditional customers. Established designer Yves Saint Laurent would eventually manage to merge street fashion and haute couture for his elite clientele. He adapted such functional items as the

One of the most controversial First Ladies of the twentieth century, Hillary Rodham Clinton displayed a preference for substance over style that often generated criticism from the fashion press.

peacoat to the needs of high society and acknowledged the hippie movement with such garments as an exquisitely fashioned patchwork wedding gown. But young designers like Quant rejected the traditional couture hierarchy altogether. Endeavoring to design for the masses rather than for a select group, radicals like her helped loosen the grip of haute couture on the reins of style. Rather than issuing fashion edicts to their clientele, these designers instead found inspiration on the street, among the people who would in turn buy their creations. While powerful clients such as the Duchess of Windsor had always had final say on their high-fashion ensembles, haute couture designers of the 1960s saw their power as arbiters of fashion wane among the general fashion-buying public.

As fashions during the 1960s and 1970s began to incorporate diverse influences and sources, the role of fashion magazine editors, whose blessings and reprobations could make or break trends, began to diminish. Legendary editors like Diana Vreeland, whom Camille Paglia has called "one of the great, stentorian dragon ladies of the century," began to disappear from the

The British invasion of the 1960s introduced American women to the miniskirt—created by English designer Mary Quant (above)—and to Twiggy (background), the reed-thin model who was the precursor of today's supermodel.

cultural landscape. Fashion was no longer restricted to a single look; it became as varied as the tastes of the buying public. Encouraged for the first time to search for her own "essence" and to create a unique self-image, a woman could pick and choose elements from popular fashions to suit her lifestyle. This new sense of self-expression represented a watershed in the evolution of twentieth-century fashion. The notion of a single fashion blueprint imposed from on high was gone forever.

The fashion establishment has finally begun to catch up with the times. Eleanor Lambert, who in 1940 created the International Best Dressed List, found it necessary to change the entire format of her poll. In the days when the list was first created, there was an accepted sameness to fashion, making it easy to single out ten women who could best represent and interpret the prevailing style; in the Modern era, this formula doesn't work. Today, the best-dressed list is divided into twelve subcategories, encompassing both classicists and mavericks. Oscar de la Renta reflected on this shift: "Elegance today doesn't mean what it did thirty years ago, when what was elegant to you and me was also elegant to everyone else. The word now has many uses; it is much more democratic, to a wider range of women. There have been divisions in society, and each phenomenon has its own icons. What is very wonderful downtown will be like a freak party elsewhere. There are so many different ramifications."

Few public figures exemplify the dizzying variety allowed by modern fashion better than Madonna. In the 1980s, when she wore see-through lace tops with dark-colored bras, tube skirts rolled down to the hip, high heels, and layers of long necklaces, teenage girls went wild, thrilled at both the sexiness and accessibility of this new look. Madonna projected the image of an independent woman who subverted patriarchal structures and retained control of her career in a predatory, male-dominated industry.

In *Guilty Pleasures: Feminist Camp from Mae West to Madonna*, Pamela Robertson credits much of Madonna's success to society's reduced attention span. She proclaims Madonna "the video generation's

elegant lilac taffeta Dior gown embellished with jet trim and embroidery. The woman who had once popularized thrift-shop apparel was flirting with classic haute couture. While the mass conversion to Evita-inspired 1950s chic that Seventh Avenue hoped for never occurred, several of its signature components did find their way into the late-1990s fashion vernacular.

Madonna is also one of the few female celebrities who can consistently steal the spotlight from that most enigmatic invention of the 1990s—the supermodel. Descended from a handful of famous models of past eras—among them Dovima, Suzy Parker, Twiggy, Jean Shrimpton, and Lauren Hutton—the supermodels of the 1990s reached a level of fame previously reserved exclusively for movie stars. Advertisers and designers began to place the success of their products on the shoulders of this select group of women, whose extraordinary physical attributes represented a new and sometimes controversial beauty ideal. Models such as Cindy Crawford, Christy Turlington, Claudia Schiffer, and Naomi Campbell became household names, their instantly recognizable faces and figures an indispensable component of every major designer's runway shows and glossy magazine campaigns. Unlike screen stars, however, the supermodels rarely possessed a signature style they could call their own; rather, their impact on fashion was only as profound as the designs they happened to be wearing at

Barbie," citing her ability to continuously update her image and offer a new look just as we become bored with the previous one. While her later fashion incarnations have not generated the fanaticism that followed her debut, she continues to draw attention and remain one step ahead of the pack. During her years in the public eye, Madonna has tapped into a seemingly limitless source of inspiration—from junkyard chic to Marilyn Monroe to S & M to geisha. Madonna is an embodiment both of the fluidity of modern fashion and of the politics of sex and identity that fashion has necessarily come to address.

After being cast as Eva Perón in the screen adaptation of the hit Broadway musical *Evita*, Madonna took a cue from history by adopting the chic style of Dior's famed "New Look." At the Academy Awards in March of 1997, not long after the movie's release, Madonna revealed that she had definitively moved to a new plane yet again, wearing a truly

BAZAAR

Harper's

A WHOLE NEW LOOK
MELANIE GRIFFITH,
THE DUCHESS OF YORK,
THE MAYFLOWER MADAM AND

MADONNA

FEBRUARY $3.00
02

0 754724 7

any given moment. As those who employed these models grew tired of their high fees and highly publicized tantrums, the public followed suit and looked for fresh faces.

In the late 1990s, a new generation of young screen actors began pushing the supermodels off the covers of magazines, even taking their place in fashion and beauty advertisements. As actresses put aside the rock and roll—derived look that had flooded youth culture in the late 1980s and early 1990s, they began to acknowledge the value of fashion credentials as a boost to their public personae. Hollywood had always understood the importance of a marketable image, and soon there was a resurgence in the employment of professional stylists, whose primary job is to help fashion-challenged stars find the look that will propel their careers to the top.

In response to this fashion renaissance in Hollywood, magazines such as *In Style* have undertaken the task of dissecting Hollywood fashion trends, providing fans and insiders alike with the formulas essential to a given star's look. Whether it's Sharon Stone's reinterpretation of classic glamour, the 1950s retro chic of Cameron Diaz's scarves and sweater sets, or the street-savvy fashions of hip-hop queen Lauryn Hill, the ingredients for a successful look are carefully analyzed, and always illustrated with ample photographs.

The natural result of this renewed symbiosis between fashion and entertainment is an inevitable blurring of the distinction between a star's on- and offscreen personae, a phenomenon that harks back to Hollywood's golden era in the 1930s. Thus, the unofficial partnership of Hollywood and haute couture that began in the 1920s, when Chanel designed costumes for Gloria Swanson, is enjoying renewed vigor as fashion designers such as Giorgio Armani and Donna Karan are commissioned for credited costume designs on major productions. This ingenious cross-marketing brings fashion to the masses and has generated name recognition for designers who typically wouldn't be known in many parts of America.

For their part, actresses lucky enough to be seen in winning couture creations enjoy added cachet when they make the best-dressed lists that have become an annual tradition for so many magazines and tabloids.

*A*mong Madonna's recent incarnations is the geisha look, featured on the cover of the February 1999 Harper's Bazaar (left). The star is shown wearing a kimono designed by Jean-Paul Gaultier.

*P*aying homage to the diversity that is the key to contemporary fashion, stars such as Cameron Diaz, Sharon Stone, and Lauryn Hill all win kudos for their individual styles.

*Among the new generation of
Hollywood actresses, Gwyneth
Paltrow has emerged as one of the
film capital's brightest stars. Her
screen wardrobe in Emma inspired
a new revival of the Empire dress,
while the alluring pink Ralph
Lauren gown she wore to the
1999 Oscars was immediately
copied by manufacturers.*

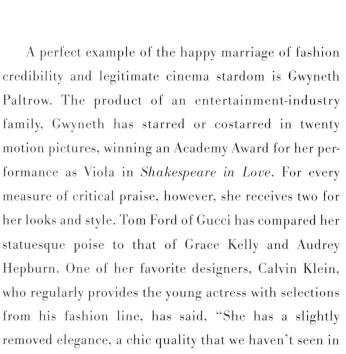

A perfect example of the happy marriage of fashion
credibility and legitimate cinema stardom is Gwyneth
Paltrow. The product of an entertainment-industry
family, Gwyneth has starred or costarred in twenty
motion pictures, winning an Academy Award for her performance as Viola in *Shakespeare in Love*. For every
measure of critical praise, however, she receives two for
her looks and style. Tom Ford of Gucci has compared her
statuesque poise to that of Grace Kelly and Audrey
Hepburn. One of her favorite designers, Calvin Klein,
who regularly provides the young actress with selections
from his fashion line, has said, "She has a slightly
removed elegance, a chic quality that we haven't seen in
a long time."

One of her amazing talents is to appear as fresh and
real in full period costume as she does in the sleek,
modern clothes she wears offscreen. Her wardrobe for
the hit film *Emma*, based on Jane Austen's nineteenth-
century novel, promoted a trend for the Empire-style
fashions of Betsy Bonaparte's era. This high-waisted,
bust-enhancing silhouette soon flooded the ready-to-
wear market, popping up perhaps most notably in Donna
Karan's collection. Gwyneth's fashion sense won her a
VH1 fashion award for best personal style in 1996, and
while this award has yet to garner the prestige of the
Oscar, it does serve as a bellwether of Hollywood fashion
trends. It definitively announced that Gwyneth Paltrow
was someone to watch closely at the end of the century—
and perhaps that a requiem for the bona fide Hollywood
fashion icon may be premature.

Among the many new faces appearing on fashion magazine covers recently, one of the most familiar to American women is that of talk-show host Oprah Winfrey, who was featured on the cover of *Vogue* in 1998. Despite the much-discussed fact that *Vogue* required that she lose an additional twenty pounds from her already slimmed-down figure for the photo shoot, the layout was received as a positive message to women: you don't have to be born with exquisite features and a flawless body to make it onto the pages of one of America's preeminent fashion magazines.

Regardless of the immediate effects of the *Vogue* appearance, Oprah Winfrey is the undisputed queen of daytime television, and one of the most powerful women in the entertainment business. Her daytime TV program is a forum for progressive, educational issues, and her female fans follow her with cult-like fascination. When Oprah introduced a book club on her program, the lucky publishers of the titles she discussed saw those books go out of stock within days.

Oprah's popularity seems to derive from a simple formula: her viewers identify with her. On camera, she is warm, gracious, witty, charming, honest, and just a bit sassy—every woman's ideal friend and confidante. Candor and personal revelation are at the heart of her show; when Oprah decided to change her life by losing the extra weight that had plagued her for years, she shared the struggle with her viewers. The low-fat recipes created for her by her private chef became a best-selling cookbook. Her motivational books and tapes encourage women to take control of their lives and move in positive new directions. Simply put, Oprah Winfrey's message is, "If you're alive, you can change."

In the years since her talk show debuted nationally, Oprah has paid consistent attention to popular fashion trends. In the 1980s, her wardrobe was dominated by the boldly colored power suits of that decade. In the 1990s, with her newly svelte physique, Oprah seems to favor the monochromatic knitwear ensembles that are fashion's current trend. And while Oprah's on-air wardrobe may not directly influence women as much as Jackie's did, her rags-to-riches life story certainly echoes that of classic Hollywood icons, and appears to have an equally mesmerizing effect on fans.

As traditional notions of fashion break down in the face of a diverse, fragmented society, it is not at all certain whether the concept of fashion icon as we know it will survive into the new millennium. Can any one woman ever again create a single signature look that will inspire a nation of followers? What is certain is that fashion is making brilliant use of the myriad channels of communication at its disposal—music, cinema, television, magazines, and the Internet. Fashion has definitively moved into the realm of democracy, where it appears content to stay.

Just as Joan Crawford inspired her fans to seek a bit of glamour in their lives, Oprah inspires her viewing public to seek spiritual and physical well-being in theirs.

Acknowledgments

For my family, for encouraging my love of fashion history

There are many people who have lent their support and advice to this project since its inception, but there are a few who must be singled out for their special contributions.

My deep thanks to Susan Wechsler, Deborah Bull, and the staff of Fair Street Productions for their enthusiasm and support. Despite the ups and downs of this project, they never wavered in their commitment to bringing *Looking for Jackie* to fruition.

Thanks also to Elizabeth Rice at Hearst Books for her interest and belief in the idea.

My agent, Jim Charlton, provided invaluable guidance, introducing me to the workings of the world of publishing and answering my endless stream of queries.

As a first-time author, I feel especially fortunate to have worked with David McAninch, a gifted editor who knew exactly how to bring the best out of my writing and shape my mountain of research into a concise body of text.

My teacher and mentor, Jean Druesedow, rekindled my enthusiasm and creative juices when this project felt overwhelming, and always knew exactly what to say to get me back on course.

I would also like to thank Gregory Wakabayashi, a talented designer, who combined and arranged the eclectic array of images we gave him into a dynamic layout that brings the thirteen women in this book to life. A special thanks also to Alice Wong, Hiro Clark Wakabayashi, and Elizabeth Kessler at Welcome Enterprises for their design and production expertise.

My dear friends Marianna Klaiman and Kathleen Maher allowed me to use them as a springboard for ideas—my brainstorming with them was invaluable in shaping this book.

The staff of the Scarsdale Historical Society supported my sabbatical at a very inconvenient time for them and the museum.

On a personal note, I could not have tackled this project without the love and encouragement of my family. My parents and sister Karen were always willing to read and critique my drafts—usually at a moment's notice. My brother Tom not only came up with the brilliant title of this book but as an author himself was there to counsel me when the task at hand seemed daunting. And, finally, I would like to express my deep gratitude to my husband, John, who, when everyone else threatened to keep away from this crazed author, stood by me and never wavered in his support.